CHRISTMAS
COOK BOOK

CHRISTMAS
COOK BOOK

TIM WILSON & REBECCA SEAL

Photography by Sam A Harris

MITCHELL BEAZLEY

CONTENTS

Introduction

Many years ago, when I first started the Ginger Pig, an old butcher said to me: 'Some customers you see once a week, some you see once a month, some you only see at high days and holidays, but at Christmas you see them all – and all at the same time!' Christmas is the busiest period in the Ginger Pig's year, and planning for the next festive season starts the moment the current one is over. Which was more popular, turkey or goose? Did beef outdo pork? And, most importantly, how many pigs in blankets did we make? (I think we are up to about 35,000, all made by hand.) We have been extremely lucky in our journey over the past 20 years. Right at the beginning I met a wonderful family, the Botterills, who farm on the borders of Lincolnshire and Leicestershire. I think my first order was for 35 turkeys and 12 geese, but now the numbers are nearer 2,000 turkeys and 1,200 geese, not to mention ducks and proper free-range chickens.

We really hope that this book of Christmas recipes offers a few tips on making Christmas cooking easier, and maybe recommends some alternatives – after all, Christmas is not just about poultry. Macaroni cheese works really well on Christmas Eve, or a slightly more adventurous melanzane parmigiana, both of which you can make in advance and then enjoy with pre-Christmas cocktails. After the big day, families and friends get together and parties are thrown, so we have included a few ideas for breakfasts, lunches and dinners for the days between Christmas and the New Year (together with a bit of advice on alcoholic and non-alcoholic drinks). For New Year's Eve itself, we have ideas for a formal dinner or a more relaxed get-together.

The meals people cook over the Christmas period are probably the most notable of the year, so it is important to us that we help our customers buy the right things – both for their own pockets and for the dishes they're going to make. We try, for example, to encourage people to buy a whole chicken instead of two chicken breasts, as it often doesn't cost that much more and will make many more meals. Traditional skills, like making stocks and using up leftovers, are vital today, with so many people feeling the financial pinch and also having a better understanding of how important it is to use the whole animal from a sustainability point of view. This really matters to us at Christmas – we don't want people spending lots of money on a big turkey only for them to have no idea how to use up the rest of it afterwards, which is why we've dedicated a whole section of this book to Christmas leftovers.

If you're already a customer at the Ginger Pig, you will know that our philosophy is about championing small producers, British farming and rare breeds. That ethos extends to how we do our own Christmases too – we want to make careful choices about all the ingredients we buy, and about making the most out of them. We hope this book helps you to do that too, while having a very happy, and very delicious, Christmas and New Year.

Tim Wilson

Essential Christmas cooking kit

A pan and meat thermometer – for ensuring meat is cooked through properly, to check whether jams and jellies have reached setting point and that oil is hot enough (but not too hot) for deep-frying.

A fat-separating jug – to remove fat from rillettes, stocks and roasting tins, when you want to keep the wonderful cooking juices for gravies and sauces.

Big saucepans with lids – Christmas often means a crowd and while you can do your spuds in two pans, it's more fuel and space efficient to do them all in one.

Big roasting tins – choose deep metal tins that will hold a whole bird, joint or porchetta and can catch their fat and roasting juices.

Heat mats – get more than you think you need. You're going to have a lot of pans on the go, and you'll need somewhere to put them.

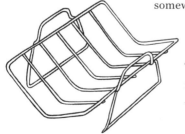

Trivet for roasting joints – to keep meat raised up out of the fat and to allow hot air to get underneath it and cook evenly.

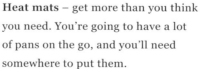

Sharp knives – if you've got a good chef's knife, keep it sharp (and keep it out of the dishwasher and stored somewhere it won't bash into other blades and get chipped or blunted). If you don't have one, pop it on your Christmas list.

A Victorinox tomato knife – this is the knife of choice for all the Ginger Pig chefs. Small, sharp and lightly serrated, it's a workhorse of a kitchen knife.

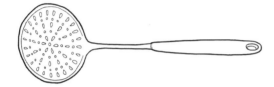

A skimmer, slider or slotted spoon – for lifting things out of fat or liquid.

Really good tongs – maybe even two pairs. For plating up, for fishing out, for arranging.

Good oven gloves – no one wants burned fingers for Christmas.

A great apron – something you won't mind wearing for most of Christmas Day (we sell rather nice ones as it happens…).

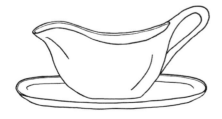

A proper gravy boat – When you've gone to the effort of making a gorgeous gravy, it's a shame to park it on the table in a Pyrex jug.

Christmas cooking timings

In advance

3 months ahead or more: Make mincemeat, chutneys, piccalilli and cranberry or redcurrant sauces.

1–2 months ahead: Book online deliveries and stock up on wine, beers and spirits. Make the Christmas cake and/or Christmas Pudding. Decide what you want to cook and order the meat.

1–2 weeks ahead: Ice the Christmas cake; make and freeze mince pies; prepare and freeze pigs in blankets and stuffing. Make and freeze gravy, or stock with which to make gravy. Check that you have all the kit you need (see pages 8–9) plus plates, glasses, cutlery, table linen and candles.

2–3 days before: Take the bird out to defrost. Make the brandy butter.

The day before

Cut any garlands or branches for table decorations. Ensure anything that needs defrosting is doing so. If you're making the goose on page 78, cook the legs today. Bake the ham. Peel and parboil the potatoes for roasting tomorrow. Prep the vegetables, put them in a bowl of water with a squeeze of lemon to prevent them from browning and store in the fridge. Work out approximate cooking times for the meat (re-weigh it with stuffing tomorrow). Make stuffing if you haven't already. Make accompaniments like horseradish sauce and bread sauce.

On the day

Draft your timetable by working backwards from when you want to eat – allow yourself at least half an hour's grace. You'll need to calculate your own exact timings, based on the recipes you're planning to cook, but here are our tips:

In the morning

If you haven't done so already, peel and parboil the potatoes for roasting, and prep other sides. Put wines or wine alternatives in the fridge to chill.

At least an hour before you want to start cooking

Remove the meat from the fridge to come up to room temperature. Add any stuffing and calculate the exact cooking time. If you're making a dish like our Festive Roast Porchetta (see page 86), allow extra time to prepare the meat and take it out 90 minutes before you want to start cooking it.

An hour before serving

Tell someone else to set the table. (Have a glass of wine.) Prep the starter.

Roast potatoes need about an hour, often at a higher temperature than the meat. If you have two ovens, that's no problem, but if not, get them started now and then crank up the heat as soon as the meat is out of the oven and resting. If your bird or joint is large, it may want up to an hour of resting.

Start cooking the vegetable sides and any vegetarian mains. (Almost every Christmas side can be warmed back up if it's ready too soon.) Warm up any pre-made sauces and bring other sauces up to room temperature.

30 minutes before serving

Get the pigs in blankets, Yorkshire puddings and anything else that takes half an hour to cook into the oven. They'll be ready just before you sit down for the starter but will happily keep warm in the cooling oven until needed.

20 minutes before serving

Pop the Christmas pudding on to steam. If you're using our recipe on page 148, it will need an hour from now until it's ready.

Warm all the serving dishes, gravy jug and plates. If you don't have space in the oven, put the plates in a washing-up bowl filled with hot water and pour boiling water into the bowls and jug to warm them up. Set out heat mats so that you've got somewhere to put everything once it's out of the oven. Check any drinks that need it are chilled and any red wines that need it are opened.

After the meal

Our only hard-and-fast rule for Christmas is that the cook is absolutely and completely exempt from doing the washing up.

Table decor

We like to keep our Christmas table as organic-looking as possible. Tim isn't a fan of crackers or tinsel and Rebecca can't stand glitter; we try to steer clear of decorations that are made of plastic or can't be recycled. And just because it's Christmas, your colour palette doesn't have to feature bright red and green. More muted, subtle combinations can also look festive (although we have seen riots of pattern that look fabulous, too). Colour combinations we like include dark green, cranberry red and dark purple; gold and white; silver and white; pastels with brass or gold; wine colours or jewel tones.

Layering fabrics is very effective – try using a tablecloth with a runner and napkins, all in complementing tones.

Forage for things that are plentiful at this time of year – pinecones and evergreens are everywhere.

Dried clementines are festive and seasonal – if making your own, slices are easier to dry, but whole ones look particularly dramatic. Set them in scallop shells, if you have some.

Use parcel tags as place cards – they look very pretty tied to foraged sprigs, particularly if you use a white pen to write the names on them.

Make cardboard or paper stars, or paper chains, using any old paper you have to hand – it's both a great activity for children and a good way to recycle.

If you want to have crackers, look for sustainable cracker kits: instead of plastic trinkets, you could give your guests flower or vegetable seeds.

Christmas wine

Tim buys wine from Thorman Hunt, a family-owned wine importer he first discovered some years ago when he was trying to track down a very specific, slightly obscure bottle of French red. They champion small independent growers everywhere from France to Lebanon and the USA, many of whom they've been working with for decades, and you'll find their wines in neighbourhood wine merchants all over the UK. There is no one better to advise on Christmas wine buying than Emma Hunt, and she has a recommendation for every chapter in this book.

'In terms of wine pairings, start by considering the array of flavours in your Christmas dinner – the roasted vegetables, the creamy bread sauce, the umami of the meat – and how your wine selection can help to enhance these dishes,' says Emma. 'Whether you want to complement the food with an equally decadent wine or prefer to contrast it with a refreshing style that can cut through the richness is your call and where the fun begins. Many merchants host wine-tasting events during the festive season, so you can try before you buy. Our ethos is very similar to that of the Ginger Pig: just as buying from independent food producers is important for the food and farming industries, the same is true of the wine trade, too. When considering your wine choices for the festive season, in the same way that a cook will want to begin with great produce, so too should the sommelier. Ask your local wine merchant to help you find wines that have been produced in the best way possible, with a focus on organic and sustainable vineyard practices – you want wines made with great grapes, with as little as possible in the way of herbicides and insecticides. These wines really showcase the grapes and their terroirs.'

Brunch

Celebrate with a glass of English bubbles – try Furleigh Estate Classic Cuvée. Husband-and-wife team Rebecca Hansford and Ian Edwards left London to buy back Rebecca's family farm and convert it into a vineyard. Similarly, Crémant is always a fantastic alternative to Champagne (it's made in the same way but in other regions of France and sometimes with different grapes, too), offering high quality at a great price. Fortnum's has a stunning, refreshing own-label Crémant from Alsace.

Nibbles, Canapés and Drinks

Gin (or non-alcoholic spirit) & Tonic. Salcombe Gin is fantastic in a G&T and the company offers an alcohol-free alternative, too: First Light & Tonic.

Starters, Platters and Boards

To compare or to contrast? It's up to you to decide. To complement the indulgent dishes with a similarly rich white, think classic Pouilly-Fuissé or lesser-known Lebanese whites such as Massaya Blanc, grown on the foothills of Mount Lebanon. Otherwise, you could cut through the decadence with a fresher option, such as a crisp rosé.

Christmas Eve

Look to the Rhône for Christmas Eve – red with the red-meat dishes, white with the white dishes. Reds from the Rhône are very food friendly. You can't go wrong with a top Châteauneuf-du-Pape, but Rasteau, Lirac or Gigondas make great nearby alternatives. The Rhône whites are textured and will complement the cheesy, creamy fish and vegetarian options.

Christmas Day

With the huge variety of foods on the Christmas dinner table, when choosing the wine go for a food-friendly, crowd-pleasing favourite. Try a Sangiovese, like a Rosso di Montalcino, whose earthy flavours will go well with the roast veg. For a more unusual but equally delicious pairing, head to the Roussillon, where Wendy Wilson, winemaker at Le Soula, produces a fresh, savoury and refined orange wine, beautifully fragrant with an almost marmalade-y orange peel flavour.

Boxing Day

A bit like a good curry, doesn't the Christmas Day feast somehow taste even better the following day? Crete's lesser-known Dafni grape makes for an ideal Boxing Day wine. The wonderful notes of bay leaf and rosemary of this unique grape variety perfectly complement the cold cuts.

New Year's Eve

Some traditions just can't be messed around with. As the festive season draws to a close and a new year dawns, raise a toast with a glass of grower Champagne – that is to say, Champagne made and bottled by the estate where the grapes were grown.

Sweet Things and Puddings

Opt for France's answer to Portugal's port with a glass of Maury – essentially, Christmas pudding in a glass.

BRUNCH

Panettone French toast

Although we serve this at brunch, you can also serve it as a dessert – in which case you could do worse than spooning a scoop of vanilla ice cream on top, along with the maple syrup or some caramel or chocolate sauce. In France, French toast is called *pain perdu*, or 'lost bread'.

Serves 4
Takes 25 minutes

4 eggs

2 tablespoons mascarpone

4 tablespoons milk

¼ teaspoon ground cinnamon

1 teaspoon vanilla extract

a small knob of butter

flavourless oil, for frying

4 thick slices of panettone, ideally slightly stale, halved

maple syrup, to serve

Set the oven to a low heat, and gently warm 4 plates in it.

Whisk together the eggs, mascarpone, milk, cinnamon and vanilla extract until completely smooth.

Place a small knob of butter and a small splash of oil into a frying pan set over a medium heat. When the butter has melted, swirl the fat around to cover the base of the pan.

Dip a piece of panettone in the egg mixture, turning to coat thoroughly, but allowing the excess to drain away. Hold the panettone carefully as even when stale it quickly becomes soft and fragile. Place in the hot frying pan and cook until golden brown on the bottom (if you have a large pan, you should be able to do at least a couple of pieces at a time).

Use tongs and a spatula to turn the panettone and cook until deeply golden on the other side, cooking each piece for a total of about 4 minutes. If the panettone is still wet in the middle, cook for slightly longer.

Repeat until all the slices have been dipped and cooked, keeping the cooked pieces warm in the oven. Serve straight away, with maple syrup drizzled all over.

Eggs Benedict, Florentine or Royale

Technically, Eggs Florentine should be served with a mornay sauce, which is a cheesy béchamel, but it's become very common to simply wilt the spinach and serve with warm hollandaise, of which we approve (see page 22 for a clever new method of making hollandaise). You can combine the toppings – spinach goes very well with smoked fish, or with ham.

 GET AHEAD You can poach the eggs in advance – you could even cook them the day before. Follow the instructions opposite to cook the eggs, then immediately plunge them into a bowl of iced water. Store, still in the water, in the refrigerator. When ready to serve, heat a pan of water until it is almost too hot to touch, but definitely not boiling. Place the eggs in the water and leave for 1½–2 minutes. Remove with a slotted spoon and drain well before serving.

Serves 4
Takes 15–20 minutes

8 eggs

2 teaspoons lemon juice or vinegar

4 English muffins, split

butter, for spreading

freshly made Easy Hollandaise
(see page 22)

For Eggs Florentine

250g (9oz) fresh or frozen whole leaf spinach

a knob of butter

a squeeze of lemon juice

salt

freshly ground black pepper

For Eggs Benedict

4 slices of good-quality cooked ham, prosciutto, Parma ham or jamón

For Eggs Royale

4 slices of sustainably sourced smoked trout or smoked salmon

Set the oven to a low heat, and gently warm 4 plates in it.

If making Eggs Florentine, place the spinach in a small pan with a lid. Add a splash of water and set the pan over a medium heat. Cover and cook until the spinach has wilted. Drain the spinach very well in a sieve, squeezing out the excess water with the back of a spoon. Tip it back into the pan and add the butter, lemon juice and a little salt and pepper. Keep warm until ready to serve.

If making Eggs Benedict or Royale, bring the ham or fish up to room temperature before serving.

Poach 8 eggs. Sieve each raw egg first, to get rid of the trailing bits of white that collect in the cooking water, then scoop out the remaining white and yolk gently with a large spoon. You can either poach 2–4 at a time in a large saucepan, or if you want to cook and serve all of them at the same time, fill a roasting tin with freshly boiled water and set it over a medium heat. Once simmering, you can use this to cook all 8 eggs together. Before adding the eggs, acidulate the water with a squeeze of lemon or a little splash of vinegar. Cook for 2–4 minutes until done to your liking. Drain the cooked eggs on a plate lined with kitchen paper. Pat the tops dry and trim away any trailing bits of egg with a sharp knife.

Toast the muffins, then butter them (keep the others warm while you toast the rest, or do them all at once under the grill). Place 2 muffin halves on each plate, add the spinach, ham or fish, then place a poached egg on each half. Spoon over the warm hollandaise and serve immediately.

Easy hollandaise

This 'reverse' hollandaise technique was invented by J Kenji López-Alt, a food-science writer for Serious Eats, who experiments with new ways to make old recipes. It is far easier and far less likely to split than the traditional method, which involves heating the yolks first. Save the whites for the pavlova on page 154.

Serves 4
Takes 15 minutes

250g (9oz) salted butter, cut into small pieces

4 egg yolks

4 teaspoons lemon juice, plus more as needed

1 teaspoon white wine vinegar, plus more as needed

salt

Place the butter in a small pan set over a medium heat and melt.

Meanwhile, place the egg yolks, lemon juice, vinegar and 1 teaspoon of cold water in a small cup or jug, into which you can snugly fit the head of an immersion blender – it won't emulsify if you use a bowl. Blitz until smooth and combined.

Once the butter is bubbling merrily, remove from the heat and allow to cool just until the bubbles subside. Spoon 1 teaspoonful of hot butter into the cup and run the immersion blender until the butter is completely combined with the yolk mixture. Repeat 3 times. The butter will emulsify into the egg yolks. Now, you can drizzle the warm butter into the cup with the immersion blender running – you might need an extra pair of hands for this, to hold the cup still. The milk solids will have settled in the bottom of the pan; omit this from the sauce. The mixture will thicken and form a rich hollandaise.

The sauce will probably be a little thick at this point, in which case gradually add 2 or 3 teaspoons of cold water, or more, to thin it. Next, taste the hollandaise. Depending on your butter, it may need a little more salt, or it could need a little more lemon or vinegar, but add them very conservatively, tasting as you go.

Use on the day you make it, ideally straight away, as once chilled, it can't easily be warmed up again. (We have, however, had success using a microwave on the defrost setting – see page 92.)

A proper fry-up

Fry-ups can be quite stressful, so don't offer your guests too many options. Cooking scrambled, fried and poached eggs all at the same time can be a recipe for a nervous breakdown, unless you run a café for a living. As Tim notes, when he does a fry-up for his partner Nicky, he still seems to use both hobs on the Aga, two of the ovens and all the pans he owns. (He likes to serve a few fried potatoes as well, or some bubble and squeak – see page 130.) If you want to save time on plating everything up, serve all the components family style in the centre of the table, and let people help themselves. To make life really easy, serve poached eggs and cook them in advance (see page 20).

If you don't fancy fried bread, just serve toast. To avoid serving your fry-up with cold toast, or being stuck making toast while everyone else tucks in, start making and buttering the toast while the meat cooks, and keep it warm in the oven alongside everything else.

Serves 4
Takes 50 minutes

flavourless oil, for frying

4 good-quality chunky pork sausages

12 cherry tomatoes, halved around the middle

a knob of butter

50g (1¾oz) chestnut mushrooms, roughly chopped

1 sprig of thyme

4–8 rashers of bacon

250g (9oz) black pudding, sliced into 4 pieces about 15mm (⅝ inch) thick

1 tablespoon duck or goose fat

4 slices of bread, halved into triangles

400g (14oz) can good-quality baked beans

4–8 eggs

salt

freshly ground black pepper

Set the oven to a low heat, and gently warm 4 plates in it, plus a dish for the cooked sausages and bacon. Start with the ingredients that take longest to cook and can wait, keeping them warm while everything else cooks.

Pour a splash of oil into a wide frying pan set over a medium heat. Add the sausages and cook gently, turning often, until golden brown all over. Push them to the side of the pan and continue to cook them for about 8 minutes or more, depending on their thickness. Once cooked through and deep brown all over, place in the oven to keep warm.

Meanwhile, add the halved tomatoes to the pan, cut side down, and cook until charring and beginning to collapse. Remove these too, and keep warm alongside the sausages.

Place a smaller pan over a medium heat and add the butter. Once melted, add the mushrooms and thyme and sauté briskly, turning often, until the mushrooms are golden and any liquid they've released has evaporated. Season with salt and pepper, then place in the oven to keep warm.

While the mushrooms cook, wipe out the sausage pan, add another splash of oil, then add the bacon. Fry it gently until crisp, turning often. (You could also cook the bacon under the grill.) Place in the oven to keep warm.

Add the sliced black pudding to the pan, adding a splash of oil if necessary, and cook for 2–3 minutes a side. Again, place in the oven to keep warm.

If you have 2 frying pans, you can start the fried bread before the meaty things are cooked. If not, wipe out the black pudding pan now and add some of the duck or goose fat. Turn the heat to medium-low. When melted, add as much of the bread as will fit in a single layer and cook for about 2 minutes a side. When golden brown and crisp, pop it in the oven. Repeat, with more bread and more fat, until all the bread has been fried.

Warm the beans in a small saucepan.

Finally, cook the eggs. Reheat poached eggs, if using, or wipe out the frying pan or pans and gently fry 1 or 2 eggs per person in flavourless cooking oil, or a knob of butter. Begin serving up by transferring the cooked eggs to the warmed plates.

Fill each plate with a rasher or 2 of bacon, a sausage, some cherry tomatoes and mushrooms, some fried bread, a slice of black pudding and a little scoop of beans. Serve straight away, with freshly brewed coffee or tea, orange juice, some salt and pepper for the eggs, and plenty of brown sauce and tomato ketchup.

NIBBLES, CANAPÉS AND DRINKS

Scotch quails' eggs

We are almost as well known for our beloved Scotch eggs as we are for our sausage rolls. Even though Scotch quails' eggs are smaller than their hen counterparts, they're still fairly filling, so if you want to serve these as a starter or canapé, you could cut them in half and serve hot, perhaps with a little scoop of our piccalilli (see page 126) on the side.

Unless you are well practised at shelling quails' eggs, we recommend buying a few extra. If you want 12 Scotch eggs in the end, cook 14–15 eggs, because unless you're very lucky, a couple will split and burst as you shell them. To shell quails' eggs, tap gently once or twice on a hard surface, then very gently roll back and forth to break the shell all over. The membrane is relatively thick compared to the shell, so use your nails to break the membrane and then very gently peel off the shell. The first few will feel very fiddly, but you'll get more confident quickly. Don't try to peel off the shell in large pieces as this will put too much pressure on the egg, and it will burst.

You can make these in advance and reheat in the oven for 5 minutes at 200°C (400°F), gas mark 6, but the yolks will set. If you want them soft, cook them just before you want to eat.

Makes 12
Takes 1 hour 10 minutes

12–15 quails' eggs

600g (1lb 5oz) sausagemeat

flavourless oil, for frying

100g (3½oz) plain flour,
plus more as needed

2 hens' eggs, well beaten

50g (1¾oz) panko breadcrumbs,
plus more as needed

Set a pan of freshly boiled water over a medium heat and bring back to a simmer.
Fill a bowl with iced water. Place the quails' eggs gently into the boiling water and cook
for exactly 2 minutes before removing with a slotted spoon and placing into the iced
water. Once cooled, peel off the shells.

Divide the sausagemeat into 12 patties, 8cm (3¼ inches) across and about 8mm
(⅜ inch) thick. Some cooks like to use a piece of clingfilm to shape Scotch eggs, laying
the patty on top, putting the egg in the centre and pulling up the meat around it, but we
prefer the control you get from using your hands. Place a patty in your palm and place
an egg in the centre, then gently enclose the egg. Form the whole thing into a ball with
no egg white visible. Place on a tray and repeat with the other eggs, then pop in the
refrigerator to chill for 10 minutes.

When ready to cook, place a high-sided saucepan over a medium-high heat and add
about 6cm (2½ inches) of cooking oil. Leave to heat up. Meanwhile, line up 3 bowls:
fill one with the flour, one with the beaten egg and one with the breadcrumbs.

Use a pan thermometer to check the oil temperature. It needs to be about 180°C (350°F).
If you don't have a pan thermometer, drop a cube of bread into the oil: if it fizzes and
browns in 30 seconds, the oil is just right.

Roll the Scotch eggs first in the flour, then coat thoroughly in beaten egg, then roll in the
breadcrumbs. Cook 2 or 3 eggs in the hot oil for 5–6 minutes, by which time they should
be golden brown all over, cooked through and with a runny yolk in the centre. You can
use the pan thermometer to check the sausagemeat temperature: insert it less than 1cm
(½ inch) into a Scotch egg so as not to break the egg. It should read 68°C (155°F) or
more. Return to the hot oil if not.

Bring the oil back up to temperature between batches, but don't let the oil overheat as
it warms back up, otherwise the breadcrumbs will crisp up before the meat has a chance
to cook.

Lift the cooked Scotch eggs out using tongs or a slotted spoon and drain on a plate
lined with kitchen paper. Serve warm, or at room temperature, with mustard, piccalilli
or a tart little winter salad.

Beetroot and goats' cheese crostini with thyme and lemon

A classic combination of flavours, and perfect for a traditional Christmas. Roasting beetroot at home always tastes best, but to save time you can use ready-cooked beetroot (not in vinegar), well drained and patted dry with kitchen paper.

Makes 20
Takes 1 hour

150g (5½oz) whole raw beetroot

125g (4½oz) soft rindless goats' cheese

2 tablespoons thyme leaves

lemon juice, for squeezing

salt

For the maple walnuts

3 tablespoons chopped walnuts

2 teaspoons maple syrup, plus more for drizzling

For the crostini

200g (7oz) baton of rustic bread (sourdough is good, or anything sturdy and robust)

mild-tasting olive oil, for brushing

Preheat the oven to 200°C (400°F), gas mark 6.

Scrub the beetroot to remove any dirt, then wrap them loosely but completely in a sheet of foil, with a pinch of salt. Roast-steam the beetroot for 50 minutes, or until tender to the point of a knife – small beetroot may take slightly less time. Remove from the oven, unwrap and allow to cool.

While the beetroot are roasting, cook the crostini. Cut the bread into 20 rounds about 1cm (½ inch) thick. Brush each side with olive oil and arrange on a baking sheet. Place in the oven and cook for 8–12 minutes, or until golden and crisp. Remove from the oven and set aside to cool.

Place the walnuts in a small dry frying pan set over a medium heat. Cook, tossing often, until they begin to smell toasty. Remove from the heat, add the maple syrup and toss to coat. Set aside.

Rub or cut the skins away from the cooked beetroot, then roughly dice them.

Spread each crostino base generously with the goats' cheese. Place 3 pieces of beetroot on top, then sprinkle over the walnut pieces, pressing both gently into the cheese so they don't fall off. Sprinkle over the thyme leaves, then pour a little maple syrup onto a spoon. Drizzle it sparingly over each crostino. Finally, squeeze over a little lemon juice.

Pear, prosciutto and goats' cheese canapés

Lovely sweet-and-salty bites, with a savoury kick from the crispy fried sage leaves. Bring everything up to room temperature before serving. If you can't find good-quality breadsticks, serve everything on crostini instead (see page 30).

Makes about 40
Takes 35 minutes

3 pears	**For the crispy sage leaves**
7 slices of prosciutto or Parma ham	a generous knob of salted butter
150g (5½oz) log of rinded goats' cheese (choose one with a mild and creamy flavour)	40 sage leaves
40 artisanal mini breadsticks (Spanish-style picos breadsticks work very well)	

For the crispy sage leaves, place a small frying pan over a medium heat and add the butter. When it foams, tilt the pan to spread it out, then add the sage leaves. Fry until the leaves are crisp and the butter is browned, about 4 minutes, then tip out into a small bowl.

You can peel the pears now, or once sliced up, whichever you find easiest. Cut the pears into halves, then cut each half into 8 wedges. Slice out the core, then halve each wedge crossways. Slice off the skin now, if you haven't already.

Place a piece of ham on a board and slice it lengthways into 3 strips. then cut each strip in half across the middle.

Cut the goats' cheese log into 20 discs, about the thickness of a pound coin, then halve each one.

To assemble the canapés, place a breadstick, a piece of pear, a piece of cheese and a crispy sage leaf on a strip of the ham. Wrap the ham around to secure, and place on a serving platter. Continue until all the cheese is used up, cutting more ham strips as you go. Serve straight away.

Blinis with smoked salmon, fennel and capers

It's hard to imagine Christmas without smoked salmon (although smoked trout is more sustainable, if you can find it). If you choose smaller cocktail blinis, you will be able to make more than 18.

 GET AHEAD Make a couple of hours in advance, omitting the fennel and the herbs, and refrigerate. But be sure to remove from the refrigerator at least 30 minutes before serving, as being very cold will dull their flavour. Add the herbs, lemon and seasoning just before serving.

Makes 18
Takes 20 minutes

4–5 heaped tablespoons soured cream (if you like things tart) or crème fraîche (if you prefer a more mellow flavour)

18 good-quality blinis

4 tablespoons very finely chopped fennel bulb

3 tablespoons capers, drained and roughly chopped

100–125g (3½–4½oz) sustainably sourced smoked salmon or trout

3 tablespoons finely chopped chives

2 tablespoons finely chopped dill

lemon juice, for squeezing

salt

freshly ground black pepper

Place a small spoonful of soured cream or crème fraîche on each blini, then add a little of the chopped fennel and capers. Arrange a small strip of the smoked fish on top of the cream, then sprinkle over the chopped chives and dill. Finish with a squeeze of lemon, a pinch of salt and a twist of freshly ground black pepper.

Ginger Pig Christmas sausage rolls

Tim Wilson, founder of the Ginger Pig, started farming with three Tamworth pigs – Milly, Molly and Mandy. At the time, prime cuts were most in demand, leaving him with plenty of high-quality meat. That meat sparked his interest in sausages, which then became our famous sausage rolls. They cause quite serious queues outside the shops at lunchtime!

These Christmas sausage rolls are big and hearty, but slice up well to make a wonderful canapé or snack with drinks, or can be served as part of a meal. We love them with our piccalilli (see page 126), or a smear of mustard. If you want the dark glaze ours have, use two beaten yolks rather than a whole egg.

Makes 6
Takes 1¾ hours, plus 1 hour chilling

450g (1lb) butter, chilled	**For the filling**
a pinch of salt	900g (2lb) Cumberland sausagemeat
2 tablespoons white wine vinegar	150g (5½oz) grated parsnip
225–275ml (8–9½fl oz) ice-cold water	75g (2¾oz) grated carrot
600g (1lb 5oz) pasta, pastry or 00 flour	2 tablespoons very finely chopped parsley
1 egg, beaten	120g (4½oz) Stilton cheese, crumbled
	60g (2¼oz) bacon, finely chopped

For the pastry, melt 50g (1¾oz) of the butter, then combine it with the salt, vinegar and 225ml (8fl oz) of the ice-cold water. Mix the wet ingredients with the flour, stirring to create a smooth dough, adding a little more water if necessary. As soon as the dough is smooth, seal in a reusable sandwich bag, or in clingfilm, and pop it in the refrigerator for an hour to chill.

Place the remaining butter between 2 sheets of baking paper and roll out into a rectangle just over 1cm (½ inch) thick. Roll the chilled dough out to form a rectangle slightly more than twice the size of the rolled-out butter. Unwrap the butter. Place the butter in the centre of the pastry and fold over the pastry to completely enclose the butter. Gently roll out so that the pastry forms a rectangle roughly the same size as it was before, avoiding touching it with your hands as much as you can – the aim is to keep the whole thing as cold as possible. If it starts to look shiny or greasy, put it back in the fridge for 10 minutes.

Fold the pastry as you would a letter, so it's a third of the size. Roll out again and repeat this letter-like folding 4 more times, chilling for 20 minutes after the first 2. Place the pastry in the refrigerator until ready to use.

Put all the filling ingredients into a large bowl and mix together thoroughly – the easiest way to do this is with your hands.

When ready to cook, preheat the oven to 180°C (350°F), gas mark 4. Roll out the pastry to form a rectangle roughly 48x28cm (19x11 inches) – it will be quite thick. Arrange the meat in a thick sausage along one of the long sides of the pastry, about 4cm (1½ inches) from the edge. Brush the edge with beaten egg, then pull the rest of the pastry up and over the sausage, to enclose it. If there is a little too much pastry overhanging, trim it off, leaving the 4cm (1½ inch) edge intact. Use the tines of a fork to press the join together firmly.

Cut into 6 equal-sized sausage rolls, then brush all the exposed pastry with beaten egg.

To cook the sausage rolls, choose a baking sheet with a rim. Line it with baking paper, then arrange the sausage rolls on it, leaving a little space between them. Unless you are very experienced with puff pastry, you will almost certainly see some butter leaking out during cooking, in which case you may want to put another tray underneath to catch any overflow.

Bake the sausage rolls for 55–60 minutes, turning the tray for the final 10 minutes or so, to ensure even browning. The sausage rolls are ready when the pastry has puffed up and is golden brown all over, including underneath.

Serve warm or at room temperature, with some piccalilli or Dijon mustard.

DRINKS

GET AHEAD All the still cocktails on the following pages can be made a day in advance and kept chilled in the refrigerator.

Bloody Mary

Serves 1

125ml (4fl oz) good-quality tomato juice

60ml (4 tablespoons) vodka

1 tablespoon lemon juice

½–1 teaspoon horseradish sauce (optional)

a generous pinch of celery salt (or ordinary salt)

2 dashes of Worcestershire sauce

3–6 dashes of hot sauce, to taste

freshly ground black pepper

ice, to serve

1 celery stick, to garnish

Make your Bloody Mary in a jug with some ice – this means you can control the heat, salt and pepper. Mix all the ingredients together, being conservative with the added flavours. Taste and adjust as needed. Strain out the used ice and serve in a tall, ice-filled glass, with a celery stick.

Spicy margarita

Serves 1

This recipe lends itself to scaling up to a jug for 6. If you make a jug in advance, be sure to stir it before serving, as the chilli will sink to the bottom, making the last serving like rocket fuel.

45ml (3 tablespoons) tequila or mezcal

30ml (2 tablespoons) Cointreau

25ml (1 tablespoon plus 2 teaspoons) lime juice

7.5ml (1½ teaspoons) simple syrup (50:50 blend of sugar and water)

a dash of Angostura bitters

a pinch of hot chilli powder

ice, to serve

For the salt rim

flaky sea salt

½ teaspoon hot chilli powder

1 lime wedge

For the salt rim, cover a small plate with flaky sea salt, then add the chilli powder and mix well. Taste a tiny pinch – it should be warmly spicy, but not overwhelming.

You can serve this drink in cocktail or wine glasses. Rub half the rim of each glass with the lime wedge, then dip the wet glass into the chilli salt, creating a salt rim on just half the glass.

Stir together the liquid ingredients in a jug, then add chilli powder to taste. It shouldn't be painfully hot, but the chilli should add warmth. The cocktail should be balanced – sweet, sour and with a kick.

We serve our margaritas on the rocks (ice) as it's easier than shaking them for a big group, so fill the glass with ice and add the margarita mixture.

Mulled wine

Serves 6–8

sliced peel from 1 unwaxed lemon

sliced peel from 1 unwaxed orange

juice of 1 orange

2 bottles of red wine

150g (5½oz) sugar, plus more to taste

12 cloves

4 green cardamom pods, bruised

1 cinnamon stick

a dusting of freshly grated nutmeg

3cm (1¼ inches) fresh root ginger, sliced

4 star anise

500ml (18fl oz) water

Place all the ingredients in a pan set over a medium heat and gently warm the mulled wine, without letting it boil. If you have a pan thermometer, don't let it get hotter than about 70°C (158°F) as the alcohol will begin to evaporate, and definitely don't let it boil. Turn the heat to very low and allow to infuse for 20 minutes. Taste and add more sugar if needed. Serve in heatproof glasses or mugs, leaving the spices and peel in the pan.

Rebujito

Serves 1

60ml (4 tablespoons) dry sherry

100ml (3½fl oz) lemonade or limeade

ice, to serve

1 lemon slice, to garnish

Fill a tall glass with ice, then add the sherry and top with lemonade. Garnish with a slice of lemon. (Other delicious variations include sweet or dry sherry with tonic, or a 50:50 mixture of dry sherry and sweet vermouth topped with soda water or lemonade and orange bitters. We also love white port and tonic. Garnish any of these with an orange slice or zest.)

Ginger Pig Boulevardier

Serves 1

We sell pre-mixed bottles of our own Boulevardier, which you can drink as is, or mix with tonic, or with tonic and Prosecco. Make a single serving or scale up to a jug for 6.

30ml (2 tablespoons) bourbon whiskey

30ml (2 tablespoons) white vermouth (we use Dolin Blanc Vermouth)

30ml (2 tablespoons) Campari

ice, to serve

1 slice of orange zest, to garnish

Stir all the ingredients with cubed ice in a jug, to chill the liquid thoroughly. Fill a rocks glass with fresh ice, then strain the liquid into the glass. Garnish with a slice of orange zest. Serve immediately.

Negroni

Serves 1

30ml (2 tablespoons) gin

30ml (2 tablespoons) sweet red vermouth

30ml (2 tablespoons) Campari

ice, to serve

1 orange wedge, to garnish

Pour all the ingredients into a rocks glass filled with ice, add the orange wedge and stir briskly, to chill everything down. If making a batch, stir together the liquids, then pour into ice-filled rocks glasses. Serve immediately. (To turn this into a Negroni Sbagliato, omit the gin, top up with 75ml (2½fl oz) of Prosecco and serve in a tall ice-filled glass.)

Champagne cocktail

Serves 1

1 brown sugar lump (or 1 teaspoon brown sugar)

1 dash of Angostura bitters

1 tablespoon Cognac

chilled Champagne (or dry sparkling white wine), to top

1 maraschino cherry or twist of lemon zest, to garnish

Place the sugar in the bottom of a Champagne flute, then add a dash of Angostura bitters. Pour over the Cognac, then carefully fill the glass with sparkling wine. Garnish with the cherry or lemon twist and serve immediately.

Kir Royale

Serves 1

1 tablespoon crème de cassis

chilled dry sparkling wine, to top

1 frozen blackberry or twist of lemon zest, to garnish

Pour the crème de cassis into the bottom of a Champagne flute, then tilt the glass slightly and gently pour in the sparkling wine. Garnish with the frozen blackberry or lemon twist. (If you prefer this still, make it into a Kir by using dry white wine instead.)

Mulled apple juice

Serves 6–8

1.4 litres (2½ pints) cloudy apple juice

sliced peel from 1 orange

juice of ½ lemon

10 cloves

4 green cardamom pods, bruised

1 cinnamon stick

a dusting of freshly grated nutmeg

3cm (1¼ inches) fresh root ginger, sliced

3 star anise

Place all the ingredients in a large pan set over a medium heat until warm, but not boiling. Allow to infuse for at least 10 minutes, then serve in heatproof mugs or glasses.

Alcohol-free drinks

It's important to cater for people who aren't drinking but still want grown-up drinks. One of Tim's favourites, based on a cocktail that Langan's brasserie used to make with gin, combines lime and mint cordial (made by Robinsons), pink grapefruit juice and tonic water.

Here are a few tried-and-tested products, all of which have found their way into Rebecca's drinks cupboard.

Natureo white, red and rosé wines – unlike many de-alcoholized wines, these are not thin or sugary, but have a decent amount of body and are great with food.

Floreale by Martini – a white vermouth alternative with a lovely floral bitterness; great with tonic. (Also available as red vermouth, Vibrante.)

Noughty sparkling white and rosé – terrible name, but a very good alternative to sparkling dry white and rosé wines.

Seedlip Spice, Seedlip Grove and Seedlip Garden – while not fake gins, these are great with tonic as an alternative to gin.

Gin-ISH – the ISH company make really good dupes for various spirits and Gin-ISH is impressive. (Rum-ISH is delicious in mocktails, and they have also released an agave-based drink to use like tequila, as well as a range of canned cocktails.)

Aecorn Bitter – an excellent substitute for Campari, although it's very, very bitter, so you can use much less. Aecorn Dry is a nice sub for dry vermouth.

Sipsmith FreeGlider – this is one of the most convincing gin replacements on the market.

Beer and ale – Rebecca likes the range produced by Big Drop Brewing Co., especially the Paradiso Citra IPA; the Days Brewing Company range; Athletic Brewing Company range; Free Damm lager; Birra Moretti 0%; Doom Bar Zero Amber Ale; Peroni Nastro Azzurro 0.0% lager; and Tiny Rebel Tropica Non Alc IPA.

STARTERS, PLATTERS AND BOARDS

Pork belly and rabbit rillettes

Our pâtés and rillettes have always been very popular – in the run-up to Christmas, we sell lots of pâté de campagne, duck rillettes and traditional chicken liver pâté. Rillettes keep well and make a fabulous gift if you're going to be a guest over the festive season, so it's worth making more than you need for a single meal.

 GET AHEAD Rillettes can be made a day or two in advance of serving in ramekins, or a week in advance if you store in sterilized jars. Once chilled, keep the ramekins in a lidded plastic box or sealed sandwich bag, in the refrigerator, to prevent any other foods tainting the flavour.

Makes 3 x 400g (14oz) jars, or up to 12 ramekins plus a jar or so leftover
Takes 4½ hours, plus 4–6 hours chilling

1 rabbit, jointed	a generous pinch of fennel seeds
750g (1lb 10oz) pork belly with bones, rind removed but fat left on, cut into large chunks	⅛ teaspoon ground allspice
	a pinch of freshly grated nutmeg
1 sprig of thyme, lightly crushed with your fingers	a generous dusting of black pepper
1 small sprig of rosemary, lightly crushed with your fingers	1 teaspoon flaky sea salt, plus more to season
1 bay leaf, torn in half	90ml (3fl oz) pork fat, goose fat or lard, melted
12 juniper berries	250ml (9fl oz) dry white wine

Preheat the oven to 130°C (260°F), gas mark ½–1.

Tuck the rabbit pieces into the bottom of an ovenproof casserole dish with a close-fitting lid. Place the pork pieces, fatty sides up, on top of the rabbit.

Tie the thyme, rosemary and bay leaf into a scrap of clean cooking muslin, and place this into the dish as well. Put the juniper berries and fennel seeds into a mortar and bruise lightly with the pestle, then tip into the dish. Add the allspice, nutmeg, pepper and salt, then spoon over the fat and pour in the wine.

Cover the dish with its lid and place in the oven. The mixture will need to cook for about 4 hours, but set a timer for 45 minutes, and when it goes off, check that the meat is covered with just enough liquid. It's not a problem if the fat on the pork belly is poking out, but make sure the rabbit is covered, adding a splash of water if necessary.

If you're not serving the rillettes immediately, sterilize 3 x 400g (14oz) clean jam jars with lids by placing in the oven for 15 minutes. If you want to serve some of it in the next day or two, you can divide it between 12 ramekins (or fewer) and put the remainder in a jar or jars.

After 4 hours, both meats should be meltingly tender. Carefully remove the hot dish – which will be full of scalding liquid! – from the oven. Use tongs to lift the meat from the pan and place it in a bowl, removing the bones as you go. Shred the meat thoroughly, using 2 forks.

Let the liquid cool slightly, then sieve it into a fat-separating jug, or regular jug, discarding the solids. Once separated, pour off the stock, or spoon off the fat, and reserve both. Put the fat in the refrigerator to thicken up.

Add enough of the reserved stock to the meat to moisten and flavour it, but don't make it wet – aim for the texture of a spreadable but coarse pâté. Taste the rillettes and add more salt and some black pepper, as needed – it's worth over-seasoning as when cool, the flavour will be much more muted, plus salt helps preserve the meat for longer. (You can also add more nutmeg or allspice.)

If jarring the rillettes, divide it between the sterilized jars and press down very, very firmly, squashing out any air bubbles (these can encourage spoilage). Pour or spoon a layer of the separated and slightly cooled fat over the top to create a seal. Seal with the sterilized lids and leave to cool before storing in the refrigerator. Technically, they should keep for a couple of weeks, but we recommend eating within a week of making.

Alternatively, if serving in the next day or two, divide individual portions between ramekins and press down neatly. Spoon a little fat over the top.

Place the jars or ramekins to chill in the refrigerator. The rillettes need to chill for 4–6 hours before serving, to firm up, but bring up to room temperature for 20 minutes before eating.

Serve with crusty bread, thin slices of toasted baguette or sourdough, and cornichons to cut through the fat. Rillettes are also very good with pickles like piccalilli (delicious but definitely not traditional) or a little wholegrain mustard.

Baked Camembert with rosemary, thyme and garlic

It's not easy to serve this dish elegantly, but it's so delicious that your guests really won't mind. To use up the scraps of remaining pastry, cut it into small star shapes, brush with beaten egg and dust with freshly grated Parmesan. Bake for 10 minutes, alongside the Camembert.

Serves 4–6 as a starter or 2 as a main
Takes 50 minutes

1 sheet of ready-rolled all-butter puff pastry

1 whole Camembert

leaves from 1 sprig of rosemary

2 cloves of garlic, thinly sliced

2 teaspoons thyme leaves

1 egg, beaten

a pinch of flaky sea salt

redcurrant jelly or cranberry sauce, to serve

Line a baking sheet with baking paper. Preheat the oven to 200°C (400°F), gas mark 6.

Unwrap the sheet of pastry and lay it out on a board. Place the Camembert on it and score 2 large discs into the pastry, one about 3cm (1¼ inches) larger than the cheese to form the base, and the other about 6cm (2½ inches) larger, to form the top – check that the second piece will be big enough to hang down over the cheese on all sides and meet the pastry base. Cut the 2 discs out, using a sharp knife.

Use the sharp knife to cut small slits all over the top of the cheese. Poke the rosemary leaves and slices of garlic into the holes. Scatter the thyme leaves over the cheese. Place the cheese onto the smaller of the 2 pastry discs on the lined baking sheet, and brush the edge of the pastry with beaten egg. Place the larger disc on top of the cheese and press the pastry edge down to meet the base. Pleat the edges to make a neat join, or press together with the tines of a fork. Cut 2 small slits in the centre of the pastry top, to allow steam to escape, then use the sharp knife again to score a pithivier-style pattern on top: gently cut a curved sun-ray pattern into the pastry, without cutting all the way through. Brush the whole thing with beaten egg and sprinkle over a pinch of sea salt.

Place in the hot oven and bake for 25 minutes. When golden brown all over and nicely puffed up, remove it from the oven. Leave to stand for 5 minutes before serving, which – because the cheese will melt voluptuously – is best done at the table on a serving platter, and in front of your guests. Place the redcurrant jelly or cranberry sauce on the table, so that everyone can help themselves.

Potato cakes with hot-smoked trout, apple and dill

Smoked trout is a much more sustainable alternative to salmon. Hot-smoked fish goes so well with these crispy potato cakes and the tart pop of flavour from the apple. If you have a couple of potato cakes left over, save them for breakfast – reheat in a warm oven, or in a frying pan, and eat with a fried egg.

Makes about 20 or serves 6 as a starter
Takes 50 minutes

	For the topping
500g (1lb 2oz) white potatoes	125ml (4fl oz) full-fat crème fraîche
1 large onion, peeled	1 tart green apple, sliced into wafer-thin crescents and placed into a bowl of water with a squeeze of lemon juice
25g (1oz) dried breadcrumbs	
2 eggs, beaten	
½ teaspoon flaky sea salt, plus more as needed	4 fillets of hot-smoked trout (or sustainably sourced hot-smoked salmon or mackerel), roughly flaked
freshly ground black pepper	finely chopped dill
flavourless oil, for frying	finely chopped chives
	a squeeze of lemon juice

Grate the potatoes using the coarse side of a grater (there's no need to peel). Keep the onion whole and grate it holding the root end. Tip the onion and potato onto a clean tea towel, wrap the mixture firmly and then squeeze out the liquid over the sink. Place the mixture in a bowl and add the breadcrumbs, beaten egg and seasoning. Stir together.

Set a large frying pan over a medium heat and add about 5mm (¼ inch) of cooking oil. Set the oven to a low heat, to keep the potato cakes warm. When the oil is hot, drop a little nugget of the mixture into the pan, cook for a few minutes and then taste to check the seasoning. Adjust if necessary. When you're happy with it, use a dessertspoon to scoop portions of the mixture into the pan, flattening them gently to form patties 6cm (2½ inches) across. Cook for about 3 minutes a side, until tanned golden brown. Drain on a plate lined with kitchen paper, and keep warm while you cook the rest.

When ready to serve, top each potato cake with a teaspoon of crème fraîche. Place 2 apple slices into the crème fraîche, then add a couple of pieces of the flaked fish. Once each cake is topped, sprinkle with the dill and chives before ueezing over a little lemon juice. Finish with a twist of black pepper and serve straight away.

Whipped squash with roasted garlic, thyme and feta

This is garlicky, so if garlic is not your jam, leave it out, or use just one or two cloves. If you're not serving this for small children, a pinch of chilli flakes or a drizzle of chilli oil is a great idea.

Serves 6–8
Takes 1 hour 10 minutes

1 butternut squash or medium pumpkin

2 tablespoons extra virgin olive oil, plus more for brushing

a pinch of salt

a twist of freshly ground black pepper

1 head of garlic

75g (2¾oz) feta cheese, crumbled, plus more to serve

3 tablespoons thyme leaves (or the crispy fried sage leaves on page 32), plus more to serve

roasted pumpkin seeds, to serve (optional)

crostini or sliced pitta or flatbreads, to serve

Preheat the oven to 200°C (400°F), gas mark 6. Remove the top of the squash or pumpkin, just enough to cut away any stem. Cut it in half and scoop out the seeds. (You can save these to roast, if you like.) Score the inside of the flesh in a criss-cross pattern, being sure not to cut through to the skin. Brush the cut sides of the flesh with olive oil and sprinkle with a pinch of salt and some pepper. Halve the garlic head crossways and brush the cut sides with a little olive oil. Place the squash and garlic on a baking sheet and roast in the hot oven for 40–45 minutes.

Remove the garlic from the oven and set aside to cool. Test whether the squash is cooked with a sharp knife – the flesh should be tender and offer very little resistance. Return to the oven for 5–10 minutes if needed. Remove from the oven and set aside with the garlic, to cool.

Use a spoon to scoop the cooked flesh away from the squash skin and place in the bowl of a food processor or the jug of a high-powered blender. Pop the roasted garlic cloves from their skins and add to the squash along with the olive oil and the feta. Blitz until completely smooth.

Serve at room temperature (not chilled) as a dip with strips of warm pitta or flatbreads or on crostini, with some extra feta crumbled over and sprinkled with the thyme (or crispy sage) leaves and some roasted pumpkin seeds, if liked.

Tim's prawn cocktail

This recipe is based on the one Tim makes at home, although he eschews the traditional hot sauce, and likes his prawn cocktail with added sun-blush tomatoes. He uses a 50:50 mixture of Hellmann's mayo and Heinz mayo, which he says gives a perfectly balanced, tart but creamy sauce.

Tim always buys the most sustainable prawns he can find. If you want large prawns, they generally come from warm waters and it's harder to find sustainable options. Avoid big wild prawns and look for organically farmed prawns or those with the Aquaculture Stewardship logo (ASC) or that have been certified by the Marine Stewardship Council. Smaller wild or farmed prawns from cold-water fisheries in places like the North Atlantic are more likely to have been certified as sustainable – the Marine Conservation Society website has detailed advice about exactly which to buy.

Serves 6
Takes 20 minutes

2 Little Gem lettuces, shredded	**For the Marie Rose sauce**
6 heaped tablespoons diced mango	275ml (9½fl oz) good-quality mayonnaise
6 heaped tablespoons diced cucumber	3 tablespoons tomato ketchup
450g (1lb) sustainably sourced cooked peeled prawns	3 dashes of Worcestershire sauce
a pinch of paprika, to serve	6 tablespoons double cream
	lemon juice, for squeezing
	Tabasco or other sour-spicy hot sauce, to taste

Whisk together the sauce ingredients, then taste and add more lemon juice or hot sauce if needed.

Arrange the lettuce, mango and cucumber in the bases of 6 large wine or stemmed cocktail glasses and spoon over half the sauce. Arrange the peeled prawns on top, then spoon over the rest of the sauce – Tim's advice is to be generous with it. Finish with a pinch of paprika and then serve.

How to build a festive cheese board

We opened our second shop on Moxon Street next door to Patricia Michelson's fabulous cheese shop, La Fromagerie, in Marylebone, London. There is no one better qualified to tell us how to serve and care for cheeses at Christmas, so here is Patricia's expert advice.

Take your cheese seriously – it will enhance the whole meal if you do. But on Christmas Day itself, no one wants a big cheese board. Just bring out a beautiful piece of Stilton or Cheddar right at the end, after the Christmas pudding. When children dash off to play with their toys, the grown-ups can sit around the table and bring out the port or Madeira, and tuck into just a little bit of cheese.

The cheese board really comes into its own on Boxing Day, with all the other cold dishes, or if you're having people over for drinks during the festive season. When making your selections, think of the five key families of cheeses. Number one, a light and creamy goats' cheese. Two, a soft cheese. Three, a hard cheese. Four, a washed-rind cheese. And finally, a blue, like a Stilton or Stitchelton. This gives you a lovely progression of flavours.

Eat your cheeses in order. Think of the flavours as starting off light and savoury, with that salty tang of the goats' cheese to set off the tastebuds. Then have something a little crumbly, like a Wensleydale or Lancashire, which also has that salty tang as a back note, followed by your brie or similar. Then go on to the hard cheese. If you don't want a traditional Cheddar, go for a Comté or Gruyère, Pecorino or Manchego. Next, the washed-rind cheeses, those stinky ones that are gorgeously creamy and mellow – things like French Livarot, Italian Taleggio or English Rollright. The blue cheese with its steely-edged veins comes right at the end, and brings together all the flavours that are in your mouth. Building up the flavour profile as you are tasting makes the journey of the cheese board absolutely delicious, and you'll enjoy everything else on the table as well.

You don't have to stick to particular cheeses, or only to British cheeses, in your selection. If instead of Stilton you want to bring out a French cheese like Roquefort or a Spanish cheese like Picos Blue, absolutely do that. There are other British blues that are extraordinary during winter, too – Beenleigh Blue, which is made from sheep's milk, Harbourne Blue, which is a goats' cheese, and Devon Blue, all three of them from the Devon creamery, Ticklemore Dairy. Alternatively, if you've got favourites from Italy or Spain or further afield, you could combine those with something more traditional. At New Year, I like to bring out a Scottish cheese board.

Raw almonds are the hidden gem of accompaniments. With the skin on, they give a creamy nuttiness that works tremendously well with cheese. Walnuts, roasted hazelnuts and pecans are wonderful with blue cheese. I pop them in little pockets among the cheeses on the board itself, which is very attractive. Apples and pears are really good too, as are dates. Grapes look marvellous, but are not always terribly tasty at this time of year. I love to have some quince paste (membrillo) for sweetness, and piccalilli (see page 126), of course, with Cheddar.

As for biscuits, keep the flavour as clean as you can, and avoid anything too salty or indeed cheesy. At La Fromagerie, we make our own, including a spelt biscuit that is not too sweet, and a caraway one, which is perfect with blue cheese. Both have just the right amount of snap – a biscuit is really just a platform for the cheese to sit on, so it can't be crumbly. Alternatively, a rustic French-style bread works very well. Sourdough is too overwhelming in terms of flavour, but a walnut bread or walnut-and-raisin bread would also be very good.

Mrs Kirkham's
Lancashire

Camembert
aux truffes

Sinodun Hill
goats' milk
cheese

Comté d'Estive

Roquefort

Petit Munster

There's no such thing as a bad wine to pair with cheese – you can enjoy it with either white or red wine, with port (ruby or tawny) or sherry – but do avoid anything fizzy, as it won't do your tummy much good (and neither will tea or coffee, or hot drinks in general). We also love cider with cheese, and for anyone not drinking alcohol, a really good-quality apple juice is an excellent partner.

Storing cheese well, so that it lasts throughout the festive season, is very simple, especially if you buy proper farmhouse cheeses, because they haven't been kept in very cold conditions and so are quite sturdy. They can last for hours out of the fridge. My go-to storage solution is easy: plastic containers. Have a separate one for each of your five families of cheeses, so that you can store like with like. Line each box with a slightly dampened clean cloth. Wrap the cheeses in clean double-layered sheets of wax paper or greaseproof paper (make sure to label each cheese!), not in clingfilm. Clip on the lid and you've created a little humid chamber, just like in our cheese room. Store the boxes in the refrigerator, with the blue cheeses at the top, where it's coldest, and the hard cheeses lower down. Alternatively, you can keep them in the garage or shed, safe in their boxes, if the weather is cool enough.

About an hour before you want to serve it, remove the cheese from the fridge, still wrapped up, and place it on the board, then cover it with a damp tea towel. About 15 minutes before you want to eat, uncover and fully unwrap the cheese. After the meal, wrap everything up again in the same way, using clean paper. This might seem wasteful, but once oxygen gets to it, the paper gets bacteria on it, and you don't want that on the cheese.

If you find there's a little furry film growing on the cheeses, don't be scared – it means it's a good cheese. Just scrape it away, very lightly, with the back of a knife. We call this refreshing the cheese and do it all the time. Cheeses kept like this will last 10 days, or even more if they're hard cheeses.

A whole truckle should be wrapped in paper, then cloth, and kept in a box – a cardboard box is fine – somewhere dry and cool.

How to build a charcuterie board for Christmas

For an Italian-style charcuterie board, we recommend choosing some speck, coppa, Parma ham, mortadella and pancetta, as well as perhaps some sliced cold porchetta (see page 89) and 'nduja. Gemma Aston, our head deli chef, loves fennel salami, finocchiona, as well. Serve with crostini sticks, focaccia or ciabatta, along with some good-quality olives and sun-dried tomatoes. Gemma's family is Italian and they serve cured meats with long slices of aubergine or courgette, griddled and then marinated in garlic-and-chilli-infused olive oil.

We sell lots of the wares for an English charcuterie board – cold cooked ham, sliced roast pork or sliced roast beef, and piccalilli.

We also sell a range of French dried saucisson, which are lovely with cornichons. Get a couple of different styles – we love the classic saucisson with fennel, or one with hazelnuts, truffles or wild boar. They look great served whole on a board, with a few slices cut from the end. Serve with a good-quality baguette, and a herbed butter made with freshly picked thyme leaves and sea salt.

Wild boar saucisson

Classic saucisson

Prosciutto

Salami

Coppa

Mortadella

You can, of course, mix up products from different countries – we like to add Spanish jamón or chorizo to our charcuterie boards, and we are also very happy to combine cheese (see page 52) with ham, especially if we're serving a smaller group.

If you're planning to store cured meats, it's better to buy things like saucisson – which will keep nicely, unwrapped and at room temperature, for several days – or whole pieces of cooked meats like ham, and then cut them as needed. Sliced ham, pork or beef won't keep for long without discolouring, although cured sliced meat will keep better.

When arranging meats ready to serve, folding the slices gently looks prettier than laying everything out flat, as does breaking up the arrangement with bread or olives. However, if you don't have a big board, or a table big enough for a board to fit onto it, don't worry – either serve as a grazing board starter before the meal, with drinks and standing up, or do as Gemma's Italian family does and pre-plate a selection for each person.

MAINS

Christmas Eve fish pie

For many of us, it wouldn't be Christmas Eve without fish pie. If you like, you can add 4 hard-boiled eggs, roughly chopped, and/or a handful of dill to the sauce along with the fish.

 GET AHEAD Assemble the pie, ready to cook, 24 hours in advance.

Serves 6–8

1 hour 40 minutes

800ml (1 pint 7fl oz) milk

600g (1lb 5oz) undyed sustainably sourced smoked haddock

250g (9oz) trout fillets (or sustainably sourced salmon)

10 peppercorns

a pinch of freshly grated nutmeg

1 bay leaf

2 sprigs of flat leaf parsley, plus 2 tablespoons finely chopped leaves

1.75kg (4lb) white potatoes

125g (4½oz) butter, plus more as needed

75g (2¾oz) plain flour

4 tablespoons single cream

1 tablespoon lemon juice

2 tablespoons capers in brine, drained and roughly chopped if large

200g (7oz) raw peeled prawns

salt

black or white pepper

Place the milk in a large pan set over a medium heat and bring up to a simmer. Add the haddock, trout (or salmon), peppercorns, nutmeg, bay leaf and parsley sprigs, and poach the fish in the milk for 6–8 minutes, or until it is just beginning to flake and fall apart.

Meanwhile, peel and roughly chop the potatoes. Set another large pan, this time filled with freshly boiled water, over a medium heat and when simmering, add the potatoes and a pinch of salt. Cook until tender, then drain and mash with a large knob of butter. Set aside.

Place the 125g (4½oz) of butter in a saucepan and set over a low-medium heat. Once it's melted, add the flour and cook, stirring, for a couple of minutes, or until the flour smells nutty; don't let the mixture brown.

Use a sieve to strain the fish out of the milk and set the fish aside (discard the bay leaf, peppercorns and parsley). Gradually add the warm milk to the butter-flour mixture (or roux), stirring continuously – this avoids lumps. Once everything is combined, continue

to cook gently, stirring often, until you have a smooth, slightly thickened sauce. Add the cream, lemon juice, capers and finely chopped parsley.

If you're making this a day in advance, cook the prawns in the white sauce now, so that you're not chilling raw fish alongside cooked – add the prawns to the finished sauce and cook for about 3 minutes longer, or until the prawns are pink and cooked through.

Taste the sauce and season with salt and pepper, if needed. White sauces are best seasoned with a small amount of white pepper, but if you don't have it, season generously with black pepper, instead.

Grease a large ceramic baking dish (ours is 24x34cm/9½x13½ inches). Flake the fish, removing any skin or bones, and arrange it in a layer across the bottom of the dish. If eating the pie straight away, add the raw prawns now, then pour the white sauce over the fish. Smooth the fish mixture out so that it sits in an even layer. Spoon the mashed potato over the pie. Once the pie is covered, smooth it with a spatula or the back of a large spoon to create an even layer. Then use the tines of a fork, dragged back and forth across the potato, to gently roughen the surface so that it crisps up during cooking. Dot the top of the pie all over with little scraps of butter. If making in advance, cover the dish and chill in the refrigerator until ready to cook.

Preheat the oven to 180°C (350°F), gas mark 4. Cook the pie for 40 minutes, or until golden brown and the filling is bubbling around the edges. Serve with buttered wilted greens, and peas.

Ginger Pig venison bourguignon pie

This is a beautiful and hearty option for a Christmas Eve supper. You can make one large pie (about 21cm/8¼ inches across and 9cm/3½ inches deep), which will serve four; you can make two smaller pies and cook them both; or you can cook one smaller pie and freeze half the filling and half the pastry, both uncooked, to use later. (And thank your past self profusely when you're eating the saved pie in the depths of dreary January.)

Serves 4
Takes 4½ hours

flavourless oil, for frying

1kg (2lb 4oz) venison shoulder, diced into 3cm (1¼ inch) pieces

2 onions, chopped

2 carrots, diced

400ml (14fl oz) beef stock, plus more as needed

500ml (18fl oz) red wine

90ml (3fl oz) port

2 tablespoons thyme leaves

100g (3½oz) smoked bacon lardons

100g (3½oz) chestnut mushrooms, roughly chopped

1 fat clove of garlic, crushed

2 tablespoons cornflour

2–3 teaspoons redcurrant jelly

1 egg, beaten

salt

freshly ground black pepper

For the pastry

1 egg, beaten

200ml (7fl oz) water

500g (1lb 2oz) plain flour

½ teaspoon salt

250g (9oz) beef suet

Place a large pan with a lid over a high heat and add a splash of oil. Thoroughly brown the venison all over, turning it regularly and working in batches if necessary. Add the onions to the pan and allow them to soften and begin to brown. Add the carrots, beef stock, red wine, port, thyme and a pinch of salt and pepper. If the meat isn't covered by the liquid, add a little more stock, or water. Bring up to a simmer, then cover and cook until the venison is tender, which could take up to 3 hours. (You can also do this in the oven, in an ovenproof pan with the lid on, at about 160°C/325°F, gas mark 3, or in a slow cooker set to high.) Check the liquid levels every 45 minutes or so.

Once the meat is tender, add another splash of oil to a frying pan set over a high heat. Sauté the bacon briskly, then when the bacon is browned and the fat is beginning to render out, add the mushrooms to the pan, adding a little more oil as needed. Turn the heat to medium and sauté until the mushrooms are beginning to caramelize. Add the garlic and cook, stirring, for 2 minutes.

Return the venison pan to a medium heat on the hob. Add the bacon, garlic and mushrooms to the venison and stir well. Bring the mixture up to a simmer, and cook for 10 minutes.

Place the cornflour in a small bowl. Spoon about 2 tablespoonfuls of the cooking liquor into the bowl and stir until the cornflour mixture is smooth. Pour this mixture into the meat pan, stirring the sauce as you do so, and cook for another 5 minutes or so, or until the sauce has thickened. Add the redcurrant jelly and stir well, then taste and adjust the seasoning or add more redcurrant jelly.

When ready to cook, make the pastry. Whisk the egg into the water, then sieve out any lumps. Place the flour, salt and suet into the bowl of a stand mixer and combine, running the beaters on slow. Next, gradually add the water (you might not need all of it), mixing until a soft dough is formed. As soon as it comes together, tip it onto a floured board or clean work surface dusted with flour, and use your hands to bring it into a ball of fairly smooth dough. Don't overwork the pastry as it may shrink during cooking.

Preheat the oven to 180°C (350°F), gas mark 4.

Divide the dough into 2 balls. Flour a rolling pin and roll 1 dough ball out to a rough disc about 35cm (14 inches) across and about 4–5mm (¼ inch) thick, if making a large pie.

Grease the pie tin with oil, then dust with flour. Drape the pastry over the tin, then gently work it into the corners. Where the pastry overlaps and pleats, pull away the excess and press the joins together smoothly, making sure there are no thick areas of pastry. Allow the pastry to overhang the rim of the tin by 1cm (½ inch), then trim away the excess beyond that. Brush the edge with the beaten egg.

Use a slotted spoon to fill the pie, lifting out the meat and vegetables first. Pour the liquid into the pastry shell last, being sure not to overfill it. You want to be reasonably generous, as if the pie isn't full the pastry will collapse downwards, but it also shouldn't be brimming, or the gravy will bubble out during cooking.

Roll out the other piece of pastry to the same thickness. Lay it over the pie and leave a generous 2cm (¾ inch) overhang before trimming off the excess. Pinch the 2 layers together, creating a crimped pattern as you go. Brush the top with beaten egg and decorate with Christmas shapes cut from the pastry trimmings. (If you have a decent-sized ball of pastry left over, freeze it to use as a topper for another pie.)

Place in the hot oven and bake for 50 minutes. When ready, the pie will be golden brown and slightly pulled away from the tin. Remove from the oven and leave for 5 minutes before gently turning out. Serve with some buttered greens.

Melanzane parmigiana

This is another of our dishes that becomes hugely popular in the run-up to Christmas, and it's a great vegetarian option for Christmas Eve. Even in Italy, there is dissent about whether the sauce should contain onion, or not – ours does, but it's up to you. If you prefer a smooth tomato sauce, do as deli head chef Gemma Aston's Italian mother does, and use passata rather than tinned tomatoes. (Rebecca's mum, who being from Birmingham is definitely not Italian, makes a version of this with layers of prosciutto and roasted peppers; Rebecca, who being from Oxford is not Italian either, tops hers with a layer of chunky breadcrumbs tossed in olive oil.)

GET AHEAD Like so many baked dishes, this is very good on its second day. Cook, cool, cover and chill, then reheat in a hot oven the next day, to serve.

Serves 6
Takes 2 hours 30 minutes, plus 10 minutes standing

4 aubergines, sliced lengthways into 5mm (¼ inch) thick pieces	**For the sauce**
	1 tablespoon extra virgin olive oil
100ml (3½fl oz) extra virgin olive oil, plus more to grease	1 banana shallot, very finely diced
a generous pinch of dried oregano or Italian mixed herbs	3 cloves of garlic, crushed to a purée with the flat blade of a knife
leaves from 1 small bunch of basil	100g (3½oz) tomato purée
3 balls of mozzarella, 120g (4½oz) each, torn into pieces	2 x 400g (14oz) cans good-quality chopped tomatoes
100g (3½oz) Parmesan cheese, grated, plus more as needed	200ml (7fl oz) passata
salt and freshly ground black pepper	a generous pinch of dried oregano or Italian mixed herbs

For the tomato sauce, place a large wide saucepan with a lid over a medium heat. Add the oil and then the shallot and sauté, stirring often, until soft, about 10 minutes. Then add the garlic and cook until fragrant and very slightly coloured.

Add all the remaining ingredients plus half a tomato can of water and some salt and pepper, bring up to a simmer and cook gently, stirring often to prevent sticking, for 1½ hours or until smooth and saucy. If the sauce reduces too quickly, add a splash of water every now and then. Taste and adjust the seasoning, if needed. If the sauce feels very chunky (some brands of canned tomatoes can be very slow to break down), then use an immersion blender to smooth it out.

About half an hour before the sauce looks likely to be done, heat the oven to 180°C (350°F), gas mark 4. Toss the aubergines with the oil, oregano, salt and pepper until well coated, then place in a single layer on a couple of baking sheets and cook for 15 minutes, or until lightly coloured and tender.

Leave the oven on and assemble the parmigiana. Grease a medium-sized baking dish (24x20cm/9½x8 inches) with a little oil. Start with a layer of one-quarter of the tomato sauce. Cover this with one-third of the aubergine, some of the basil leaves, and then a layer of one-quarter of both the cheeses. Repeat until the aubergine is used up, finishing with the of the tomato sauce, then the remaining mozzarella and finally a good coating of Parmesan – grate a little more if necessary.

Bake in the oven for 30 minutes, or until the cheeses have melted and browned, and the dish is bubbling. Leave to stand for 10 minutes before serving.

Ginger Pig macaroni cheese

If you want to serve a meat-free dish on Christmas Eve, you can't go wrong with this macaroni cheese, originally created by our wonderful group head chef, Yvonne Hunter. We know there's a lot of cheese in it, but the thing is, we really love cheese. There are many ways to play with macaroni cheese – feel free to skip the breadcrumb topping if you prefer. Rebecca loves the sauce with a pinch or two of English mustard and some cayenne pepper. She used to work in a restaurant that served theirs with a layer of wilted spinach in the middle, to which you could also add nuggets of blue cheese. You cannot go wrong by adding crispy bacon lardons (this is true for more or less anything). For outrageous richness, make the sauce with a mixture of 75 per cent Cheddar and 25 per cent Gruyère, and when you pour the macaroni into the baking dish, stud it with little pieces of buffalo mozzarella.

 GET AHEAD You can make this 2 days in advance, and chill or even freeze it before cooking. (Defrost for 24 hours in the refrigerator before baking.)

Serves 8–10
Takes 1¼ hours

500g (1lb 2oz) dried macaroni

a splash of extra virgin olive oil

75g (2¾oz) butter, melted (optional)

1 tablespoon thyme leaves (optional)

75g (2¾oz) panko breadcrumbs (optional)

For the sauce

1.5 litres (2¾ pints) milk

a pinch of freshly grated nutmeg

150g (5½oz) butter

75g (2¾oz) plain flour

750g (1lb 10oz) Cheddar cheese, grated, plus more to top

salt

white pepper

Cook the pasta in lightly salted boiling water for 8–10 minutes, until al dente. Drain and refresh it in cold water. Return to the pan and mix with a little olive oil to prevent sticking.

While the pasta is cooking, start the sauce. Place the milk and nutmeg in a large pan and bring up to just about boiling. Remove from the heat and set aside.

In a third large saucepan set over a low-medium heat, melt the butter for the sauce. When foaming, add the flour and cook for a couple of minutes, stirring constantly, until a smooth paste is formed. Don't allow the flour to take on any colour. Gradually add the hot milk, little by little, whisking it into the flour-butter mixture (or roux), with a pan-safe whisk. Once all the milk has been added, cook for 5–8 minutes, stirring, or until the sauce is smooth and slightly thickened.

Turn the heat right down, then add the cheese, mixing well to allow it to melt into the sauce, then remove from the heat straight away, as cooking the cheese at this point can cause it to split and make the sauce grainy. Taste and season with salt and a little white pepper. (White pepper is more potent than black, so be conservative to start with.)

Preheat the oven to 180°C (350°F), gas mark 4. Mix the melted butter with the thyme and panko breadcrumbs for the topping, if using.

Add the pasta to the cheese sauce and mix well. Grease a roughly 7cm (2¾ inch) deep, 23x30cm (9x12 inch) ceramic baking dish, or 2 smaller dishes, with a little butter or oil, then pour in the macaroni cheese. Smooth flat with a spatula, then sprinkle the panko mixture evenly over the top, or finish with a generous layer of grated cheddar.

Bake the macaroni cheese for 40 minutes, or until piping hot throughout and bubbling at the edges.

ROASTING BIRDS

If you're feeling the pressure of cooking for the hordes on Christmas Day, don't. It is a very important day and we all like to get things right, but let's be honest, the most important thing is the people that you are with. So relax, have another glass of wine and don't take it too seriously.

How to stuff a bird

Turn the bird so that the neck end (not the cavity) is facing you. Untuck the skin around the neck, untrussing it or cutting it free from any string holding the skin down. Tuck some of the stuffing under the skin, pushing it into the gap between the skin and meat. Place some or all of the rest of the stuffing into the cavity of the bird, but don't overfill it – air needs to circulate within the cavity so that the heat can penetrate the breasts from underneath, so make sure you can slide your hand into the cavity between the breasts and the stuffing.

If you have stuffing left over (a mini turkey, for example, will probably only take about 250g/9oz), grease a loaf tin and cook the remaining stuffing in the tin at around 180°C (350°F), gas mark 4, for 45 minutes or so while you finish the sides, after the turkey has come out of the oven. Or pop it in the refrigerator, uncooked, and cook it to go with a leftovers meal on Boxing Day.

To truss or not to truss?

This is really a matter of taste, says our group head chef Yvonne Hunter. If you like the neat look given by trussing the bird (using butcher's string to tie in the legs and wings), then leave it on or re-truss after stuffing, especially if you plan to serve the roasted bird as a centrepiece. The argument for trussing is that it helps retain moisture in the extremities and prevents the bird as a whole drying out. However...trussing does cut down on the amount of skin available to crisp up, by tucking some of the skin tightly in between the legs and breasts, where it cannot go brown. So, it's up to you.

Cooking times

Take the bird out of the refrigerator an hour before you want to cook it, longer if it's a big bird. Allow 30 minutes or so to get your bird ready for the oven. Allow for 30–60 minutes unexpected extra cooking time, especially if you're cooking a big bird, and if your oven is very full of other things at the same time. Then, after cooking, allow at least 30 minutes for the bird to rest before serving – this lets all the lovely juices rearrange themselves throughout the meat, and for the meat to continue cooking.

For chicken, guinea fowl, cockerel and capons, calculate the cooking time as roughly 45 minutes per kilo (2lb 4oz), plus about 20 minutes. Duck needs 20 minutes at 220°C (425°F), gas mark 7, first, then 45 minutes per kilo (2lb 4oz) of meat. (See page 81 for goose cooking times and pages 72–74 for turkey.) Whichever bird you are cooking, weigh it after stuffing and work out the cooking time from there.

Use your intuition as well as a meat thermometer to tell you whether the bird is cooked. For chicken, turkey, guinea fowl and cockerels, the meat should not be pink, the juices should be clear and the joints should feel loose when you wiggle them. (If you have a meat thermometer it should read at least 71°C/160°F when pressed into the thickest part of the leg and breast, but see page 72 for slightly different temperatures for slow-cooked turkey.) Duck, goose and game birds can all be served pink.

Baste several times during cooking.

Roast turkey with a bacon lattice

You can never have too much bacon at Christmas, but dressing turkey with a bacon lattice does a valuable job, too: it imparts flavour and helps prevent the breast drying out.

When working out your timings for the day, give yourself about 30 minutes to prepare the turkey. Take the turkey out of the refrigerator 1–2 hours before it goes in the oven. This is important to ensure even cooking – if the centre of the bird is chilled, it may not cook through. Then, allow at least 30 minutes for the turkey to rest, along with an extra 30 minutes or so leeway on the cooking time, in case it needs a bit longer.

A meat thermometer is the best way to check whether a turkey is cooked through. Officially, the advice is that it should reach 74°C (165°F), but that can result in dry meat. As long as you are cooking a good-quality, high-welfare turkey – as ours, reared by the Botterill family in Leicestershire, are – and you rest the bird for at least half an hour (during which time it will carry on cooking), and as long as it reaches 68°C (155°F) for at least three minutes in the thickest parts of the meat (deep in the breast, at the thigh-body joint and the leg-thigh joint), then any nasties should be dealt with.

At the Ginger Pig, we classify our turkeys by size as follows – choose the cooking time for your turkey's weight in the method on page 74, weighing the bird after you've added any stuffing.

Mini – 4–5kg (8lb 13oz–11lb), feeds 4–6

Small – 5–6kg (11lb–13lb 4oz), feeds 6–10

Medium – 6–7kg (13lb 4oz–15lb 7oz), feeds 10–14

Large – 7–8kg (15lb 7oz–17lb 10oz), feeds 14–18

Extra large – 8kg (17lb 10oz) or more, feeds 18+

Cooking time – depends on the size of the turkey (see page 74)

18 rashers of streaky bacon

1 turkey

salted butter

freshly ground black pepper

Make the bacon lattice 15 minutes before you're ready to cook. Find a clean surface or board and lay down a large piece of clingfilm (this will make it easier to move the lattice when complete). Lay out 9 rashers of bacon vertically and snugly together on the

clingfilm, with the fat on the right-hand side. You may need to gently pull and stretch the rashers to the same length to ensure that they lie closely together and there is enough coverage (especially if placing on a large turkey!).

Fold down the top ends of rashers 2, 4, 6 and 8, making enough room for a rasher of bacon to fit horizontally and form the top of the lattice square. Lay the first horizontal rasher across the top of those rashers remaining on the board. Return the folded-down ends of the rashers to their original positions, covering the first horizontal rasher and creating the first weave of the lattice.

Lift up the bottoms of rashers 1, 3, 5, 7 and 9, which previously remained on the board, folding them upwards at the point where they meet the first horizontal rasher. Place a second horizontal rasher across the rashers that remain flat on the board, making sure to keep it snuggled up close to the first horizontal one.

Replace the lifted rashers and repeat. Continue lifting alternate vertical rashers, placing each horizontal rasher close to the last before replacing the lifted rashers. Repeat until you've used up all the rashers and have a neat square of streaky bacon lattice.

Preheat the oven to 220°C (425°F), gas mark 7. Rub the turkey skin with plenty of butter and pepper. Gently lift the finished lattice onto the breast of the turkey. Using 2 very long sheets of foil – use more than you think you will need! – make a big tin foil cross inside a roasting tin large enough to take the turkey, place the turkey in the middle of the cross, and lift up and wrap the foil around to make a loose but closed parcel. Cook in the oven for 40 minutes.

Reduce the heat to 170°C (335°F), gas mark 3–4, and cook for a further 2½–2¾ hours for a mini turkey, 3–3½ hours for a small, 4 hours for a medium, 4½ hours for a large and 5 hours for an extra large. Baste the turkey every 45 minutes or so, working quickly so that the turkey doesn't cool down, and keeping the oven door shut to retain heat.

Uncover for the last 30 minutes to crisp the bacon, or if you prefer, move the bacon to a tray so it can crisp up as well as the turkey's skin.

If you don't have a meat thermometer, stick a long skewer in the fleshiest part to test for doneness: the juices should run clear. Rest the cooked bird for 30–40 minutes while you finish preparing the side dishes. (If you want crispy skin, avoid wrapping it in foil, as the steam will dampen the skin.)

GINGER PIG STUFFINGS

These recipes provide enough stuffing for a mini or small bird (see page 72 for our sizing guide). If you are cooking for a big crowd (more than 12 people), increase the recipe by half, or double it for an extra-large bird.

 GET AHEAD Mix the stuffing ingredients together a day in advance, cover and keep in the refrigerator, or prepare and freeze 1–2 weeks in advance.

Sage and onion

Takes 10 minutes

450g (1lb) sausagemeat

leaves from 2 bushy sprigs of sage, finely chopped

1 banana shallot, finely diced

Mix all the ingredients together.

Pork and chestnut

Takes 10 minutes

450g (1lb) sausagemeat

leaves from 2 bushy sprigs of sage, finely chopped

120g (4½oz) cooked chestnuts, very finely chopped

Mix all the ingredients together.

Prune and brandy

Takes 10 minutes, plus 4 hours soaking

110g (3¾oz) prunes, pitted and finely chopped

1 tablespoon brandy

1 heaped teaspoon soft brown sugar

450g (1lb) sausagemeat

Place the prunes in a bowl with the brandy and leave for 4 hours, or overnight. Just before cooking, stir the sugar into the mixture until dissolved, then add the sausagemeat and combine thoroughly.

Roast duck

Our ducks come from the Botterill family, who farm a piece of land on the Belvoir Estate, on the border of Leicestershire and Lincolnshire, and from whom we have been buying exceptional poultry for many years. They let their birds roam free and grow to full maturity, which means our ducks are bigger than most found in other shops.

Roughly speaking, you can cook duck hot at 220°C (425°F), gas mark 7, for 20 minutes, as below, then at 180°C (350°F), gas mark 4, for 45 minutes per kilo (2lb 4oz). So a 3kg (6lb 8oz) bird will cook in about 2 hours 35 minutes, in total, and a 2kg (4lb 8oz) duck will cook in just under two hours, but each bird (and oven) is different.

Serves 6
Takes 2 hours 20 minutes, plus 15 minutes resting

1 duck, weighing about 3kg (6lb 8oz)

salt

Preheat the oven to 220°C (425°F), gas mark 7. Arrange a rack in the bottom of a deep roasting tin. Place the duck on top and use a pin or a needle to prick the skin all over (this allows the fat to render out, and helps the skin crisp up). Remove any giblets and rub a generous amount of salt all over the duck.

Place it in the hot oven and cook for 20 minutes. Next, turn the heat down to 180°C (350°F), gas mark 4, and cook the duck for a further 1½–2 hours. Keep an eye on how much fat renders out and pools in the tin beneath. You may need to carefully pour or spoon it out once or twice during the cooking time, so that it doesn't overflow. (Don't throw it away as it's wonderful for cooking, especially potatoes. If you really don't want to keep it, do not pour it down the sink, as it will solidify and block your pipes.)

The duck is ready when you can scrape a knife over the surface of the skin and it makes a scratching noise, and the leg joints feel loose if you wiggle them. Remove from the oven and rest for at least 15 minutes before serving.

Roast goose breast and confit legs

Geese are big and can be quite tricky to cook alongside everything else on Christmas Day. Our solution is to separate the legs and the breasts, cooking the legs in their own fat a day or more before, then the breasts can be cooked much more quickly and in a smaller dish, on the day. The only slightly fiddly bit is separating the meat into legs and breasts, so if possible, get a butcher to do this for you, and ask them to retain the carcass and bones for gravy.

We love roast goose with our Sage and Onion Stuffing (see page 75) and Apple and Cider Sauce (see page 89), as well as the gravy on page 122 and all the other trimmings.

If cooking a goose that was previously frozen, defrost it in the refrigerator for at least two days, as a whole goose will not defrost overnight.

 GET AHEAD Cook the goose legs one to two days before you want to serve, and store in their fat in the refrigerator.

Serves 6
Takes 2¾ hours on Day 1, plus overnight chilling; 1½ hours on Day 2, plus 30 minutes resting

1 goose, weighing about 5kg (11lb)	2 sprigs of thyme
6 juniper berries	a strip of orange zest
4 allspice berries	flaky sea salt or fine salt
2 bay leaves, torn in half	freshly ground black pepper
8 peppercorns	

The day before you want to serve the goose, preheat the oven to 160°C (325°F), gas mark 3.

Either ask your butcher to remove the legs and separate the breasts in advance, or do it yourself with a sharp knife (see photographs on page 80). Look for the joint where the thighs join the body, and cut there. Remove the wings as well. (Remove the giblets and use them to make the poultry gravy on page 122.)

Chop off any large and visible bits of fat from around the neck, the opening of the cavity and underneath the goose and set them aside.

Cut away the back of the goose (that is, the backbone and ribs, the parts underneath the bird), leaving you with just the breasts, and set aside the bones that you have removed.

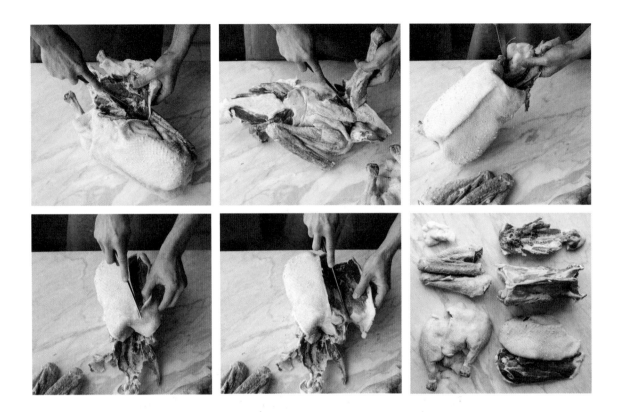

If you have a butcher's knife and some experience, you might be able to slice down the breastbone and separate the 2 breasts, but a standard kitchen knife won't do it and it's fine to leave it as one piece. Remove any bones sticking out underneath that will prevent the breasts fitting snugly into a roasting tin. Store the breasts in the refrigerator until about an hour before you want to cook them.

Place the fat, wings and the legs into a roasting tin – they should fit quite tightly as you want to cook the meat in the fat as it renders out. Add the juniper berries, allspice berries, bay leaves, peppercorns, thyme, orange zest, 1 teaspoon flaky sea salt (or ½ teaspoon fine salt) and lots of black pepper, tucking all the aromatics under the meat. Separately, put the bones into another roasting tin so that you can use them for gravy stock (see page 122).

Place both tins into the oven. Cook the bones for an hour or so, then remove from the oven and set aside or, if not using immediately, chill to use in the poultry gravy.

Cook the legs for 2¼ hours, basting once with the fat, halfway through. Remove the legs from the oven, cool until you can handle them, transfer to a dish or tub with a lid, including the fat, cool and then store in the refrigerator.

On the day you want to serve, take the legs and breasts out of the refrigerator at least an hour before you want to cook them. Preheat the oven to 220°C (425°F), gas mark 7.

Season the breasts generously all over and place on a rack set in a deep roasting tin (to catch the fat). Remove the legs and wings from their fat and place in a separate roasting tin. Spoon over a little of the fat and then season with a little more salt and pepper. Roast the breasts for 50–60 minutes, basting once halfway through, or until the skin is crisp and the breast meat is cooked (like game birds, goose can be eaten pink, but should reach an internal temperature of at least 65°C/149°F). Exactly how long this will take depends on the thickness of the breast and the temperature of the meat before it went in the oven.

Add the legs to the oven just after you baste the breasts at the halfway point. Roast them for 25 minutes, or until hot through and crisp on the outside. (You can melt, then strain the remaining leg fat and keep it for cooking roast potatoes.)

Rest both meats for 30 minutes, keeping them warm. It is essential that the breast rests, covered in foil, for this amount of time, both for the juices to redistribute throughout the meat, and for all the meat to reach a safe internal temperature.

Serve your guests a portion of both the sliced breast meat and crispy leg meat. Let people help themselves to the wings, if they like.

VARIATION Whole roast goose

If you want to roast the goose whole, remove the chunks of fat from the opening of the cavity before cooking, and any giblets. Stuff the goose as per the instructions on page 70. Season generously and cook on a rack in a large roasting tin – you may need to spoon or pour off the very hot fat during cooking, or it could overflow. Strain and keep the fat for roasting potatoes and cooking Yorkshire puddings. Our goose supplier, Botterills, recommends gently pricking the skin all over (don't prick the meat) to help the fat render out; however, this does result in slightly less crispy skin, so it's entirely up to you.

Weigh the bird after adding any stuffing and then calculate the cooking times as follows: start off by giving the goose 30 minutes at 220°C (425°F), gas mark 7, then roast for 30 minutes per kilo (2lb 4oz) at 180°C (350°F), gas mark 4. A 5kg (11lb) bird would therefore need to cook for approximately 3 hours. As with the turkey recipe on page 72, allow an extra half an hour when you plan your timings, as the meat may take slightly longer to cook. If the skin is darkening too fast, cover it with a loose sheet of foil. The meat needs to be at least 65°C (149°F) before it rests, so ideally, check it with a meat thermometer.

Allow the bird to rest for at least 30 minutes after cooking, and don't wrap in foil as this will trap moisture and make the skin soften again. Don't skip resting as the meat continues to cook during that time, and the juices will redistribute nicely, making it both easier to carve and more delicious to eat.

Rib of beef

Tim once sold a five-bone fore rib joint of beef to a couple who insisted they would eat the whole thing for their Christmas lunch. History doesn't tell us whether they succeeded, and if they did, whether they also had sides. As Tim pointed out to them, a five-bone rib weighs 7–10kg (15lb 7oz–22lb). We can only hope they put some into sandwiches like those on page 145.

This is our roasting guide for a large (two or more bone) wing or fore rib joint. If you want to be absolutely sure about how done your roast is, insert a meat thermometer into the centre: it should read approximately 50°C (122°F) for rare, 54°C (129°F) for medium-rare and 58°C (136°F) for medium. Some cooks prefer to season after cooking as the salt starts to draw out moisture, and if done too far in advance, can create a wet surface and make it harder to get a decent crust. We season in the last moments, just before the joint goes in the oven. For six people, you will need a two-bone wing rib (from the loin end), weighing about 3.5kg (7lb 11oz). Larger joints, like a fore rib with three bones (weighing about 4.5kg/10lb) will feed 6–8.

Traditionally, after an initial 25 minutes in the oven, recipes call for meat to be cooked for 15 minutes per 500g (1lb 2oz) for rare meat, 17 for medium-rare and 20 for medium. We find that 15 minutes can result in very rare meat when cooking smaller pieces. That's totally safe if that's how you like to eat it, and there will be slightly better done meat at either end of the roast for anyone who prefers their meat cooked closer to medium, but cook it for 17 minutes per 500g (1lb 2oz) if you like it slightly better done. Resting the meat is crucial as it will continue to cook as it does so.

Serve this with the Ginger Pig Red Wine Gravy on page 123, the horseradish sauce on page 121 and the Yorkshire puds on page 110.

1 large prime rib or wing rib joint (2 or more bones)	1 teaspoon mustard powder
	sea salt and freshly ground black pepper
2 tablespoons flavourless oil	

Remove the meat from the refrigerator at least 1 hour before cooking. Preheat the oven to 220°C (425°F), gas mark 7, and calculate the required roasting time:

For rare – 17 minutes per 500g (1lb 2oz)

For medium-rare – 20 minutes per 500g (1lb 2oz)

For medium – 22 minutes per 500g (1lb 2oz)

Place the joint in a deep roasting tin so that it is standing up on the bone. Pat the surface of the meat dry with kitchen paper. Using your hands, coat the surface of the joint with the oil, just enough to allow the seasoning to stick, then season with the mustard powder, salt and pepper. Make sure the oven is fully heated, then place into the hot oven and roast for 25 minutes.

When the initial searing time is up, remove the beef from the oven. Turn the oven down to 170°C (335°F), gas mark 3–4, and leave the door open for a few seconds to help it come down to temperature. Return the beef to the oven for your calculated roasting time.

When the cooking time is over, remove the tin from the oven. Allow the meat to rest in the tin for 10 minutes, then remove the meat, wrap in foil and allow it to rest for another 20. Serve the meat in slices, with plenty of hot gravy, horseradish, Yorkshires and your choice of sides.

Roast guinea fowl with fennel, shallot and white wine sauce

Ginger Pig guinea fowl are often chicken-sized, but you will often find smaller guinea fowl weighing 1kg (2lb 4oz) or so, which are perfect for smaller Christmas gatherings of two to three people. Guinea fowl are slightly gamier and richer in flavour than chicken and unlike other Christmas birds, are not prone to drying out. Leftovers make extremely nice sandwiches, or can be used in ragù (see pages 129) and shepherd's pie (see page 138).

Serves 4
Takes about 2 hours

2 small guinea fowl, about 1 kg (2lb 4oz) each or 1 large guinea fowl, about 2kg (4lb 8oz)

8 banana shallots, peeled and halved lengthways

½ small fennel bulb, trimmed and sliced widthways

3 cloves of garlic, in their skins

1 tablespoon thyme leaves

2 tablespoons softened salted butter

4 rashers of smoked back bacon, or 4 rashers of streaky

10 dried prunes, halved

350ml (12fl oz) white wine

150ml (¼ pint) chicken stock

1 tablespoon extra virgin olive oil

1½ teaspoons Dijon mustard

4 tablespoons double cream

a squeeze of lemon juice

1 tablespoon finely chopped parsley

a generous amount of salt

freshly ground black pepper

Preheat the oven to 180°C (350°F), gas mark 4. Choose a roasting tin into which the guinea fowl will fit fairly snugly. Arrange the shallots in a layer on the bottom of the tin, cut sides facing up. Top with the sliced fennel and whole cloves of garlic, and keep it all as tightly nestled together as possible, so that the vegetables sit beneath the bird or birds and cook slowly in the juices and the wine, rather than burning.

Mix the thyme leaves with half the butter. Loosen the skin of the guinea fowl around the cavity and push the herbed butter under the skin, massaging it along the meat. Rub the remaining butter all over the bird. Drape the bacon over the breasts. Tuck the halved prunes into the cavity. Place the bird or birds over the shallots and fennel.

Pour the white wine and chicken stock into the roasting tin. Season everything with salt and freshly ground black pepper and drizzle over the extra virgin olive oil.

Roast the guinea fowl for 22 minutes per 500g (1lb 2oz), plus 15–20 minutes at the end of cooking, using the liquid in the pan to baste the meat a couple of times. If the bacon slides off, don't worry, just pop it back in position – it's not really protecting the meat, but is rather there for flavour. If the bacon starts to really darken, push it into the liquid in the pan.

When the allotted cooking time has passed, check the meat is done as you would for a chicken: pierce one of the legs at thickest part and check the juices run clear. If not, return it to the oven for a few more minutes.

Lift the bird or birds from the tin and place on a carving plate. Remove the prunes and roughly chop them. Loosely cover the meat with foil and leave to rest.

Place the roasting tin on the hob and bring up to a simmer. If there's a lot of liquid, reduce it for a few minutes, to intensify the flavour. Lift the garlic cloves out and squeeze the soft garlic from the skins, then mash the cloves into the sauce. Crumble the bacon into the sauce too, discarding any rind. Stir in the Dijon mustard. Add the cream and stir thoroughly. Simmer for just a couple more minutes, then taste and add a squeeze of lemon and some more salt and pepper, as needed.

Carve the meat. Add the prunes and parsley to the sauce at the last minute, then spoon the sauce over the meat.

Festive roast porchetta

A proper porchetta is made from the boneless loin of the pig and its belly, cut so that it forms one flat, level piece of meat. It is then seasoned and sometimes stuffed, before being rolled and roasted until the meat is tender and the skin has crackled. In Italy, where it comes from, porchetta is often served as a street food, stuffed into soft white rolls. In 2022, when our farmers sadly lost their turkeys to bird flu, we created this festive roast and sold hundreds of porchettas, ready rolled.

Good crackling depends on the skin being very dry and getting a blast of heat from a very hot oven. If you can, leave the pork uncovered in the refrigerator the night before you cook it, as this will help dehydrate the skin. Don't skip patting it dry and don't stint on the salt just before cooking, either.

You can use this recipe for a smaller porchetta, just reduce the amount of stuffing, and calculate the cooking time at 170°C (335°F), gas mark 3–4, as 30 minutes per 500g (1lb 2oz).

Serves 8–10
Takes up to 5 hours, plus 30 minutes resting

1 porchetta, prepared by your butcher and with the skin scored, weighing about 4kg (8lb 13oz)	zest and juice of ½ orange
a knob of butter	a generous handful of sage leaves, finely chopped
5 shallots, finely diced	a generous handful of parsley leaves, finely chopped
150g (5½oz) soft dried apricots, finely chopped	125g (4½oz) panko breadcrumbs
125g (4½oz) dried cranberries, chopped	½ teaspoon fine salt
juice of ½ lemon	½ teaspoon freshly ground black pepper
	1 tablespoon flaky sea salt

Remove the porchetta from the refrigerator at least an hour before you start cooking. Unroll it and pat the skin dry with kitchen paper.

When ready to cook, preheat the oven to 220°C (425°F), gas mark 7 – it needs plenty of time to get really hot, or the skin won't crackle. Place a small frying pan over a medium heat. Add the butter and then the shallots and fry gently, stirring often, until translucent. Place the cooked shallots in a large bowl and add all the other ingredients, except the flaky sea salt. Mix well.

Cut 5 lengths of butcher's string (or cotton string), each long enough to wrap around the rolled porchetta and tie. Lay 4 of them vertically and parallel to each other on a clean work surface, close enough to each other that they will wrap around the rolled meat, and one along the middle of the others, at 90 degrees.

Pat dry the skin again. Place the meat, skin side down, over the strings so that one short side is facing you and the long sides are parallel to the 4 pieces of string. Season the meat generously, then arrange the stuffing on top. It will be very crumbly and a bit messy; don't worry.

Roll up the meat. If your butcher has cut the skin so that one end forms a flap, make sure that when you roll it, the flap covers the loose meat at the other end, and forms a neat join with the skin there. Don't overlap the 2 layers of skin, or the skin will become tough during cooking. Use the strings to tie the rolled meat tightly. (You may need another pair of hands for this bit.) If lots of stuffing has fallen out, push it back into the rolled porchetta.

Line a roasting tin (deep as a lot of fat will render off) with baking paper. Transfer the rolled pork to the tin. Rub the flaky sea salt into the skin, working into the score marks.

Place the porchetta into the very hot oven and roast for 30 minutes. Then turn down the heat to 170°C (335°F), gas mark 3–4, and cook for a further 3½ hours. (Use a meat thermometer to check the centre of the roast is around 65°C/149°F at this point.) If the skin hasn't turned to crackling by this time, crank the heat back up to 220°C (425°F), gas mark 7, and cook it for a further 10–30 minutes, checking every 5 minutes that the skin isn't burning. If it still doesn't crackle, you can remove the meat from the oven, cut off the string, slice off the skin and put the skin back into the oven on its own for a few minutes.

Rest the meat for about 30 minutes before serving. Because some of the stuffing will inevitably have fallen into the pan, along with a lot of fat, the pan juices are not ideal for making a gravy (which is not traditionally served with porchetta, anyway). However, the rich, juicy meat is delicious with tart-and-sweet redcurrant jelly (see page 125) or cranberry sauce (see page 124).

VARIATION Traditional Italian porchetta

If you prefer to cook your porchetta without stuffing, follow the method on pages 87–8, but use the ingredients below. Unstuffed porchetta like this is wonderful sliced up for sandwiches (see page 145), or even added to a charcuterie board (see pages 56–7). Year round, we sell a lot of sliced roast pork on our deli counters.

1 porchetta, prepared by your butcher and with the skin scored, weighing about 4kg (8lb 13oz)

4 tablespoons fennel seeds

a generous handful of parsley leaves, finely chopped

3 cloves of garlic, finely chopped

2 tablespoons freshly ground black pepper

2 tablespoons flaky sea salt

Spread the fennel seeds, parsley, garlic, pepper and half the salt over the meat. Roll, season with the remaining salt and cook following the main recipe on page 88.

Apple and cider sauce

This is extremely good with our porchettas, but also with roast duck (see page 77).

GET AHEAD Cook this up to a month in advance and freeze it.

Serves 6
Takes 35 minutes

700g (1lb 9oz) Bramley apples (or Granny Smiths), peeled, cored and roughly chopped

300ml (½ pint) sweet cider

2–4 tablespoons sugar

lemon juice, for squeezing

Place the apples and cider in a saucepan and set it over a medium heat. Bring up to a simmer and cook until the apples soften. Mash it into a sauce with the back of a spoon. Taste and gradually add the sugar and lemon juice – it should be sweet but also fairly tart. Store, covered, in the refrigerator until ready to use. Serve warm or at room temperature, but not cold from the refrigerator.

Roasted cauliflower, crispy sage, blue cheese and almonds

This is a vegetarian main dish that we've designed to fit nicely into the main Christmas feast. To make this completely plant-based, skip the cheese or replace it with a really good-quality vegan blue cheese alternative (Rebecca likes a brand called Strictly Roots), and cook the sage leaves in olive oil.

Serves 4
Takes 35 minutes

2 tablespoons extra virgin olive oil

2 teaspoons Dijon mustard

2 teaspoons wholegrain mustard

1 cauliflower, about 700g (1lb 9oz)

2 tablespoons flaked almonds

75g (2¾oz) blue cheese, at room temperature

45 crispy sage leaves (see page 32)

salt

freshly ground black pepper

Preheat the oven to 200°C (400°F), gas mark 6. Line a roasting tin with baking paper.

In a large bowl, stir together the oil, mustards and some salt and pepper. Slice away the leaves from the cauliflower, and set them aside. Break the cauliflower into medium-sized florets, cutting any large florets in half, and add to the bowl. Discard any damaged leaves, chop any large ones and then add them to the bowl. Use your hands to work the mustard mixture into the cauliflower, ensuring every piece is well coated. Tip the cauliflower into the prepared tin and place in the hot oven. Roast for 10 minutes.

When the timer goes, turn each piece of cauliflower, add the almonds to the tin and return to the oven. Cook for another 10 minutes, or until the cauliflower is tender and lightly charred, and the almonds are light gold.

When the cauliflower is almost ready, crumble the blue cheese over it and return to the oven for 3 minutes, so that it melts into the cauliflower. Top with the sage leaves and drizzle over the browned butter from the sage pan. Serve straight away.

Celeriac steaks in miso and white wine with Béarnaise sauce

The aim here is to create a meat-free main course that sits happily among all the other dishes that form part of a Christmas meal. Our vegetarian friends tell us that no matter how much they might love spicy food the rest of the time, they find it a bit baffling when they are given something flecked with chillies, cumin or turmeric to go alongside their sprouts and roast potatoes. The miso and soy used in this dish are intensely savoury, and meld with the wine, garlic and butter to make an umami-laden pan sauce.

If you're cooking for a crowd, you can cut six celeriac steaks from a good-sized celeriac, but you will need two lidded frying pans and to double up the sauce ingredients. Béarnaise can be made an hour or two ahead and kept at room temperature. It will harden if kept in the refrigerator, and is very liable to split if reheated, but we have managed to warm it to just above room temperature using the defrost setting on a microwave for 40 seconds, running it for 10-second bursts, stirring and checking its consistency each time.

To make this completely plant based, you can cook the celeriac in olive oil, skip the Béarnaise and serve with the pan sauce, or stir some black pepper and finely chopped tarragon and shallot into good-quality vegan mayonnaise.

GET AHEAD Make the celeriac steaks and the pan sauce a day in advance, keeping the celeriac slightly undercooked, cover and chill in the refrigerator. Reheat in a single layer in a frying pan, ensuring the sauce does not dry out.

Serves 4
Takes 45 minutes

1 celeriac

2 knobs of butter

a splash of flavourless oil

50ml (2fl oz) dry white wine

75ml (2½fl oz) hot water

a pinch of vegetable bouillon powder

½ teaspoon white miso paste

¼ teaspoon soy sauce

1 clove of garlic, peeled

For the Béarnaise sauce

125g (4½oz) salted butter, cut into small pieces

2 egg yolks

2 teaspoons lemon juice, plus more as needed

½ teaspoon white wine vinegar, plus more as needed

2 teaspoons finely chopped tarragon

1 teaspoon very finely chopped shallot

salt and lots of freshly ground black pepper

First, make the Béarnaise sauce. Place the butter in a small pan set over a medium heat and melt. Meanwhile, place the egg yolks, lemon juice, vinegar and 1 teaspoon of cold water in a small cup or jug, into which you can snugly fit the head of an immersion blender – it won't emulsify if you use a bowl. Blitz until smooth and combined.

Once the butter is bubbling merrily, remove from the heat and allow to cool just until the bubbles subside. Spoon 1 teaspoonful of hot butter into the cup and run the immersion blender until the butter is completely combined with the yolk mixture. Repeat 3 times. The butter will emulsify into the egg yolks. Now, you can drizzle the warm butter into the cup with the immersion blender running – you might need an extra pair of hands for this, to hold the cup still. The milk solids will have settled in the bottom of the pan; omit this from the sauce. The mixture will thicken and form a rich hollandaise.

Add the chopped tarragon and shallot, then taste and add a little more salt, lemon or vinegar, but add them very conservatively, tasting as you go. Set the sauce aside, at room temperature (unless chilling and rewarming as per the introduction).

Trim the knobbly bottom from the unpeeled celeriac and discard. Remove 5cm (2 inches) or so from the top of it. Cut 4 steaks, each just over 1cm (½ inch) thick, from the widest part of the celeriac. (Keep any remaining celeriac and use it in slaw or remoulade – see page 118.) Trim away the rough skin from each slice.

Place a wide frying pan, for which you have a lid, over a high heat. Add 1 knob of butter and a splash of cooking oil. When the butter is foaming, swirl the fats together and over the base of the pan. Place the celeriac slices into the hot pan and cook, allowing them to caramelize. After 6–8 minutes, once the bottoms are darkening (don't let them burn), turn the slices and allow the other sides to brown.

Whisk the wine, hot water, bouillon powder, miso paste and soy sauce together until smooth, then pour into the pan. Bruise the garlic, leaving it whole, and add to the pan along with the second knob of butter. Cover with a lid, reduce the heat to low and braise the celeriac for 5 minutes, then remove the lid and turn the heat up, letting the pan juices reduce. Turn each piece of celeriac in the liquid. Taste – the wine needs time for the alcohol and any tartness to bubble away, so if it is reducing too fast, add a splash of water. Add a tiny bit more soy sauce if it needs more savouriness, or a little more butter for richness. Season to taste with salt and pepper.

Check that the celeriac is tender all the way through. If the sauce needs more time to reduce, remove the celeriac from the pan and set aside. Keep everything warm until ready to serve. Serve with a little of the pan juices spooned over and a dollop of Béarnaise. Finish with a twist of black pepper.

Boxing Day glazed ham

Tim considers a good ham sandwich, made with homemade roasted ham, one of the very finest things in life. At home, his preferred glaze is marmalade, but you may prefer the Ginger Pig glaze below – choose one glaze or the other, not both.

A gammon is an uncooked ham, so if you are starting with a cooked ham, then skip ahead to the glazing part of this recipe.

 GET AHEAD A glazed ham will keep for 5–7 days in the refrigerator, meaning you can safely cook it a couple of days before Christmas, if you plan to serve it on Boxing Day.

1 gammon, plain or smoked	**For the marmalade glaze**
whole cloves, to stud the ham	100g (3½oz) fine-cut marmalade
flavourless oil, for greasing	1½ tablespoons orange juice

For the Ginger Pig glaze

250g (9oz) golden syrup

100g (3½oz) demerara sugar

25g (1oz) wholegrain mustard

1 tablespoon white wine vinegar

1 teaspoon English mustard powder

Soak the gammon in cold water for 1–1½ hours. This will get rid of any excess salt from the curing process. Preheat the oven to 180°C (350°F), gas mark 4.

Pour 3cm (1¼ inches) of boiling water into a roasting tin. Place the gammon on a rack in the tin, making sure the water doesn't touch the meat. (If you don't have a rack, use twists of foil to make a trivet for the meat.) Loosely cover the gammon with foil but ensure the foil is airtight – you may need to use a couple of pieces, crossways to each other.

Bake the gammon for 55 minutes per kilo (2lb 4oz), loosening the foil for the last 20–30 minutes of cooking. Remove from the oven.

When cool enough to handle, remove the skin (but be careful not to remove the fat as well). Your gammon is now officially a ham. Turn the oven up to 220°C (425°F), gas mark 7.

Use a sharp knife to score a criss-cross pattern in the fat, cutting diamonds about 3cm (1¼ inches) wide.

Decide which glaze you would like. Whisk together the glaze ingredients, then spoon the glaze over the ham, spreading it all over the fat. Stud each diamond with a clove.

Grease a clean tin and put the ham into it, then pop the glazed ham into the hot oven. Bake the ham for 20–30 minutes, keeping a close eye at the end of cooking, as the glaze may catch and burn. If the glaze at the top of the ham caramelizes faster, place a square of foil over it to protect it, while the rest catches up. (If the ham is on the large side, weighing more than 2.5kg (5lb 8oz), you may wish to check it has by now reached an internal temperature of 68°C/155°F, using a meat thermometer.)

Remove from the oven and set aside to cool. You can eat it hot or warm, but at Christmas, we love it cooled and sliced.

New Year's Eve chicken Wellington

Beef Wellington is more famous, but we aren't sure why – chicken Wellington is far easier to make and far less likely to overcook, while still looking fabulous.

Making a good duxelles means chopping the mushrooms and shallots very finely – it's easiest to do this with the chopper attachment in a food processor. Chilling the Wellington mid-way through making it is important because it helps to firm up the chicken once wrapped in the ham; without chilling it can lose its shape while cooking, resulting in a rather flat Wellington.

 GET AHEAD Make the Wellington a day ahead and store it, uncooked and unglazed, in the refrigerator until ready to cook.

Serves 6
Takes 2 hours, plus 2 hours chilling and 20 minutes resting

900g (2lb) skinless and boneless free-range chicken breast fillets

500g (1lb 2oz) puff pastry or 2 sheets of ready-rolled all-butter puff pastry

flavourless oil, for frying

120g (4½oz) prosciutto, Serrano or Parma ham, in long slices (long enough to wrap around and enclose the chicken)

1 egg, beaten

salt

freshly ground black pepper

For the duxelles

75g (2¾oz) salted butter

100g (3½oz) shallots, very finely minced

240g (8½oz) chestnut mushrooms, very finely minced

2 cloves of garlic, crushed to a paste

1 tablespoon thyme leaves

2 tablespoons finely chopped flat leaf parsley

For the duxelles, melt the butter in a frying pan set over a medium heat and then add the shallots. Cook gently for 5 minutes, then turn down the heat and add the mushrooms. Cook until the liquid has evaporated, about 15–20 minutes – when you move the mushrooms apart, no liquid should puddle in the pan. Add the garlic, herbs and some black pepper, and cook for another couple of minutes. Remove from the heat and set aside.

Pat the chicken dry with kitchen paper. Remove the pastry from the refrigerator. Line a large baking sheet with baking paper.

Pour a splash of oil into a large frying pan. Place the chicken fillets smooth side down in the pan and cook until lightly browned. Remove from the heat.

Roll out a large piece of clingfilm across a clean work surface. Arrange the ham slices crossways, ready to wrap the chicken with them. Spread the duxelles mixture across the ham, covering an area about 30x20cm (12x8 inches) and leaving the ends of the ham uncovered. Place the chicken on top of the ham, seared sides facing outwards, in a long sausage shape, about 30cm (12 inches) long, running at right angles to the ham – you can slice any really fat fillets lengthways to help make the sausage as even and neat as possible. Season the meat generously all over.

Bring the ends of the ham up over the chicken, overlapping them to secure, encasing the chicken and duxelles. Chill for half an hour.

If using a block of pastry, halve it and roll out to form 2 rectangles, roughly 25x35cm (10x14 inches). Place one of the sheets of pastry on the prepared baking sheet. Using the clingfilm to help you, lift and roll the chicken parcel into the centre of the sheet of pastry. Brush the pastry immediately around the meat with beaten egg. Place the second sheet on top. Tuck the pastry around the meat to form a Wellington, crimping the 2 sheets together firmly with your fingertips to seal. Trim the excess pastry away, leaving a rim of pastry about 3cm (1¼ inches) wide on all sides. Glaze the whole thing with egg.

Decorate the Wellington with the pastry trimmings if you like, then gently brush the decorations with egg. Chill for 90 minutes.

Preheat the oven to 200°C (400°F), gas mark 6. Cook the Wellington in the oven for 55 minutes. Rest the Wellington, out of the oven, for 15–20 minutes before serving.

Guard of honour with salsa verde and white bean mash

Interlacing the bones of two racks of lamb to form a guard of honour looks fancy, but is very easy to do – the ideal dish for a formal New Year's Eve dinner or another special occasion.

If you can get chunky seven-bone racks of lamb, weighing 600g (1lb 5oz) or so, you can feed 6–8 people with two of them, but if your racks are quite lean, they will feed only 4. You need two racks to form a guard of honour. We like our bean mash a bit rough and ready, as it has a nice texture, but if you prefer it smooth, just blitz it in a high-powered blender, until you get the texture you like.

GET AHEAD Make the salsa verde earlier in the day. If storing in the refrigerator, bring up to room temperature before serving.

Serves 4–8
Takes 45 minutes

2 racks of lamb, at least 500g (1lb 2oz) each

1 tablespoon extra virgin olive oil

salt

freshly ground black pepper

For the bean mash

1 tablespoon olive oil

2 onions, finely chopped

a pinch of salt

2 cloves of garlic, crushed

3 x 400g (14oz) cans cannellini or haricot beans in water, drained but not rinsed

3–4 tablespoons extra virgin olive oil

For the salsa verde

a big handful of dill leaves

leaves from 5 bushy sprigs of mint

leaves from 1 bunch of parsley

2 tablespoons finely chopped tarragon (optional)

1 anchovy fillet from a can, roughly chopped

1 clove of garlic, crushed

2 tablespoons capers in brine, drained

8 tablespoons extra virgin olive oil

1 teaspoon sherry vinegar

1 teaspoon Dijon mustard

Preheat the oven to 200°C (400°F), gas mark 6, and line a roasting tin with baking paper.

Place a large frying pan over a high heat (or use 2 pans, if necessary). Rub the lamb racks all over with the olive oil and salt and pepper. Place both the lamb racks in the hot pan, fat side down, and sear for 2 minutes, or until the fat is golden. Turn over and sear the other side for 1 minute, then stand the lamb so the bones are pointing upwards (holding with tongs if necessary) and sear for another minute. Remove from the pan and transfer to the roasting tin. Arrange the racks of lamb so that the bones stick up and each rack's bones are pointing at the other's, then interlace the bones to form a guard of honour.

Place the lamb in the oven and roast for 18–22 minutes for pink meat, depending on the thickness and meatiness of the racks. Remember that the lamb will continue to cook as it rests. Add another 5 or 10 minutes for medium or well-done meat.

While the lamb is roasting, make the mash. Wipe out the pan in which you browned the lamb and return it to the heat. Add the oil, onions and a pinch of salt, and sauté gently until translucent and just beginning to turn golden. Add the garlic and cook for 2 minutes. Add the beans and warm them through, then roughly mash (in the pan if you have a pan-safe masher) to form a rough, chunky mash. Add the extra virgin olive oil and a little water if the mash seems dry. Taste and add more seasoning and oil if necessary, remembering that the salsa verde is salty.

Traditionally, salsa verde is chopped by hand until all the ingredients meld to form a rough sauce, with the oil, vinegar and mustard added last. However, we have had success quickly blitzing everything in a food processor, but be careful not to over-process – salsa verde should not be smooth. Taste the sauce for seasoning and tartness – you are aiming for piquant, tart and fresh. If you want more savoury saltiness, add another half anchovy, finely chopped.

Remove the lamb from the oven and set aside to rest somewhere warm, for 5 minutes. Gently warm the plates.

Carve the lamb at the table and serve it and the mash on the warmed plates, with some of the salsa verde spooned over.

Slow-cooked pork shoulder stuffed with orange and prunes

Meltingly rich and tender meat, cut through with apple, orange and sweet prunes. If you can, leave the pork uncovered overnight, in the refrigerator, before cooking. This dehydrates the skin and helps make great crackling.

Serves 8–10
Takes up to 5½ hours, plus 2 hours soaking and 30 minutes resting

150g (5½oz) prunes, roughly chopped

100ml (3½fl oz) brandy

4–5kg (8lb 13oz–11lb) boneless pork shoulder, butterflied and skin scored by your butcher

flavourless oil, for frying

1 small onion, finely diced

leaves from 3 bushy sprigs of sage, finely chopped

leaves from 1 small bunch of parsley, finely chopped

zest and juice of 1 orange

1 red apple, grated

125g (4½oz) panko breadcrumbs

1 tablespoon flaky sea salt

fine salt

freshly ground black pepper

Soak the prunes in the brandy for 2 hours or, ideally, overnight.

Remove the pork shoulder from the refrigerator at least 1 hour before you start cooking. Pat the skin dry with kitchen paper.

Place a small frying pan over a medium heat. Add a splash of oil and when hot, add the onion. Sauté gently until soft, about 10 minutes. In a large bowl, mix together the herbs, orange zest and juice, apple, breadcrumbs and plenty of seasoning. Add the sautéed onion and the chopped prunes.

Line a roasting tin with baking paper and preheat the oven to 220°C (425°F), gas mark 7.

Arrange 3 lengths of string parallel on a clean work surface. Place the meat, skin side down, on the pieces of string so that you can use them to secure the meat once rolled up. Season the meat generously with salt and pepper.

Cover the meat with the stuffing mixture, then roll it up, enclosing the stuffing. Use the strings to secure the rolled pork, tying them tightly. If any stuffing falls out at this point, press it back in. Place in the prepared roasting tin.

Pat the skin dry with kitchen paper once more, then work the flaky sea salt into the skin, especially where it has been scored. Place the meat into the oven and cook for 30 minutes, then turn down the heat to 160°C (325°F), gas mark 3, and cook for 3½–4 hours.

Use a meat thermometer to check the centre of the roast is around 65°C (149°F) at this point. If the skin hasn't turned to crackling by this time, crank the heat back up to 220°C (425°F), gas mark 7, and cook for a further 10–30 minutes, checking every 5 minutes that the skin isn't burning. If it still doesn't crackle, you can remove the meat from the oven, cut off the string, slice off the skin and put the skin back into the oven on its own for a few minutes. Rest the meat for 30 minutes before serving.

Sole with caper brown butter

Often served in restaurants, a dish like this is perfect for New Year's Eve because it feels special but is also easy to achieve at home. Dover sole can be expensive, so feel free to swap for something less pricy if your fishmonger can give you another sustainably sourced flat fish. Consider fillets of brill, or Cornish or megrim sole (just ask if it's better to cook them on or off the bone). Rebecca has even done this recipe with plaice. If you can only get larger sole, ask the fishmonger to divide it into individual portions.

Serves 4
Takes 35 minutes

a knob of butter	**For the caper brown butter**
flavourless oil, for frying	150g (5½oz) salted butter
flour, for dusting	4 tablespoons capers in brine, drained and roughly chopped
4 x 300–400g (10½–14oz) sustainably sourced Dover or lemon sole	1 heaped tablespoon finely chopped parsley
salt	lemon juice, to taste
freshly ground black pepper	

First, make the caper brown butter. Cut the butter into cubes, then place in a small pan set over a medium heat. If possible, use a pan with a pale interior, as that makes it easier to see when the butter changes colour. Let the butter melt, and then it will begin to foam. After a couple of minutes, the foaming will become less agitated and the butter will begin to smell nutty and turn a golden colour. As soon as the colour changes, pour the butter out of the pan and into a small bowl, as it can quickly burn at this stage. Allow it to cool slightly, then add the capers, parsley and a squeeze of lemon. Set aside and keep warm while you cook the fish.

Set the oven to a low heat, and gently warm 4 plates in it. Set a large frying pan (or 2) over a medium heat. Add a knob of butter and splash of oil, and swirl the pan(s) to coat the base(s).

Pour some flour onto a plate and season it generously with salt and pepper. Dredge the fish or fish fillets in the flour, shaking off the excess, then place in the hot pan(s). Cook for 2–3 minutes, until golden, then carefully turn using a large spatula or fish slice, to cook the other sides for another 2–3 minutes.

Transfer the fish to the warmed plates and spoon over the caper brown butter just before serving with baby potatoes and wilted spinach.

SIDES, SAUCES AND LEFTOVERS

Roasted Brussels sprouts with bacon, chestnuts and cream

Lardons measuring about 1cm (½ inch) work best here, and you can trim away the fat if there's a lot, since this is a rich dish served as part of a rich meal. If you don't have room in the oven, you can do this on the hob instead, but you will need to blanch the halved sprouts in boiling water for a couple of minutes first. Drain, let them dry and meanwhile gently sauté the bacon and chestnuts in the oil until the lardons have crisped up. Add the sprouts and sauté until they begin to caramelize, about 4–5 minutes. Finish with a squeeze of lemon and serve with or without the cream, as below.

Serves 4
Takes 40 minutes

500g (1lb 2oz) Brussels sprouts	5–6 tablespoons single cream (optional)
3 tablespoons flavourless oil	juice of ½ small lemon
175g (6oz) smoked bacon lardons	freshly ground black pepper
125g (4½oz) cooked chestnuts, crumbled into halves (optional)	

Preheat the oven to 200°C (400°F), gas mark 6. Trim the sprouts, removing any tough stems and damaged outer leaves. Wash the sprouts, then halve the largest. Leave smaller sprouts whole, or they will become very soft during cooking.

Choose a baking sheet with a rim or a large roasting tin into which you can fit everything in a single layer. Tip the sprouts, oil, lardons and chestnut pieces, if using, into the tin and toss with a pinch of pepper, using your hands to ensure every sprout is coated in oil and seasoning. Shuffle the sprout halves so that most of them are facing cut side down.

Place in the hot oven and roast for 15 minutes. Remove from the oven and toss gently – you will notice some of the loose leaves are darkening and turning nutty in flavour. Return to the oven for 5–10 minutes, then taste one of the sprouts to check for doneness – it's up to you whether you want them completely tender or with a bit of bite.

Remove the tin from the oven. You can serve the sprouts as they are, with a squeeze of lemon and some pepper, or you can add the cream. Place the roasting tin over a ring set to a medium heat and once sizzling, add 4 tablespoons of the cream. Remove from the heat straight away and toss everything together. Add the rest of the cream if it seems dry. Squeeze over a little lemon juice and toss again, then taste and add more juice as needed – it shouldn't be lemony, but the juice should bring welcome tartness. You probably won't need salt because of the lardons. Finish with a twist of black pepper and serve.

Pigs in blankets

In Rebecca's family, the pigs were always cocktail sausages, which she still likes for their manageable size. But it's hard to get higher-welfare cocktail sausages, so she's learned to buy good-quality, thin chipolatas and twist them in the middle to create two cocktail-sized sausages. You will need to calculate the exact quantities depending on the size of your sausages, the number of guests and how many other sides you're serving. We usually go for one full-sized chipolata per person, but you could do more.

 GET AHEAD These can be prepped, covered and chilled – or cooked, covered and chilled – a day or so in advance of serving.

Serves 6
Takes 45 minutes

flavourless oil, for greasing

6 chipolatas

6 rashers of streaky bacon

Lightly grease a roasting tin. Gently twist each chipolata in half at the middle, turning them a couple of times to create cocktail-sized sausages. Use a sharp knife to separate them.

Lay a bacon rasher on a board and stretch it gently. This should help it crisp up. Cut it in half (trim off any thick bits of rind, if you like). Wrap each little sausage in the bacon, then place in the greased tin.

The pigs need to cook for 30 minutes at 180°C (350°F), gas mark 4, which you could either do in advance, reheating them for 10 minutes or so in the hotter oven while the roast potatoes cook and the meat rests, or you can cook them alongside other sides if they're cooking at the right temperature.

Yorkshire puddings

An essential side if you're serving roast beef.

Makes 16
Takes 40 minutes

200g (7oz) plain flour

3 eggs

300ml (½ pint) milk

a generous pinch of fine salt

3–4 tablespoons dripping, lard or flavourless oil

Preheat the oven to 200°C (400°F), gas mark 6 (ideally, do the puddings while the meat is resting and you're roasting potatoes or other vegetables at a higher temperature).

Whisk together the flour, eggs, milk and salt.

Place 2 x 12-hole muffin or tart trays into the hot oven and heat them up for 10 minutes, then add a little of the fat to 16 of the indentations. Use a heatproof brush to brush the fat up the sides, then return the trays to the oven to heat the fat for 5 minutes. Remove the trays from the oven and – working quickly so it all stays hot – carefully pour the batter into the tins, filling each indentation halfway. Place back in the oven immediately and set a timer for 15 minutes. Try not to open the oven at all during this time.

The Yorkshires will probably need another 5–8 minutes, but you can safely open the oven if necessary for other dishes, now. The puds are ready when they're golden brown and puffed up. Remove from the oven and if any have stuck, use a narrow spatula to loosen them from the tray. Serve warm or hot.

Honey-roasted roots

Oven-steamed and then roasted, these sweet roots are treated a little like roast potatoes. Giving them a slightly longer cooking time, with honey, allows them to soften and then caramelize deliciously.

GET AHEAD Get this ready for the oven one or two days in advance.

Serves 6
Takes 50 minutes

1kg (2lb 4oz) mixed roots – carrots, parsnips and beetroot work beautifully

2 tablespoons extra virgin olive oil

a pinch of salt

3 tablespoons runny honey

leaves from 1 sprig of rosemary

Preheat the oven to 200°C (400°F), gas mark 6. Peel the vegetables and cut into large wedges – leave the thin ends of the carrots and parsnips whole as they will burn if too thinly cut. Line a roasting tin with baking paper. Place the vegetables in the tin along with the oil and salt and toss well with your hands, coating everything in oil. Cover the tray with foil and place in the oven for 15 minutes.

Remove the foil and drizzle over the honey, then gently toss (the parsnips may already be tender and fragile). Sprinkle over the rosemary leaves and return to the oven for 25 minutes, keeping an eye that nothing is charring towards the end. Serve straight away.

Roast potatoes

If roasties don't crisp up, it's usually because they've not been cooked for long enough. Lots of recipes suggest you can crisp up a potato in half an hour, but that's not really possible – allow 50 minutes, or even an hour. Optional extras include sprigs of rosemary or thyme, or a few whole cloves of garlic, in their skins, added for the last 20 minutes or so of cooking.

GET AHEAD Peel and chop the potatoes several hours in advance, and store covered in cold water. (If you have an air fryer, you can cook them a day ahead and reheat and crisp up at 200°C/400°F for 6–7 minutes.)

Serves 6
Takes 1 hour 20 minutes

1.5kg (3lb 5oz) floury potatoes, ideally Maris Pipers, peeled and cut into large chunks

2½ tablespoons goose fat

1 tablespoon vegetable or sunflower oil

sea salt flakes, to serve

Heat the oven to 200°C (400°F), gas mark 6. Set a large pan of salted boiling water over a high heat. Bring back to the boil and add the potatoes. Simmer for 10 minutes to parboil, then remove from the heat and drain. Allow to steam-dry for 10 minutes. While the potatoes steam, place the goose fat and vegetable or sunflower oil in a roasting tin (or 2) and place in the oven to heat up.

Return the potatoes to their pan, cover with a lid and give them a shake, just enough to roughen their cut edges, which will help absorb the fat and create crunch.

Remove the hot tin from the oven and place the potatoes carefully into the hot fat. Turn each potato once or twice in the fat to coat. Return to the oven and roast for at least 50 minutes, turning them after about half an hour and then every 15 minutes or so, until they are crisp, golden brown all over and crunchy. Sprinkle sea salt flakes over to serve.

Ginger Pig gratin dauphinoise

We sell a lot of dauphinoise potatoes in the run-up to Christmas. Some cooks like to include thyme in the cream, and put cheese on top, but we love this simpler, more traditional version. Don't try this with lower-fat alternatives to double cream, as they are less heat stable, and will split.

Serves 6–8
Takes 1½–2 hours, plus 25 minutes standing

500ml (18fl oz) double cream

200ml (7fl oz) milk

freshly grated nutmeg

2 cloves of garlic, crushed to a paste with the flat blade of a knife

800g (1lb 12oz) Maris Piper potatoes, peeled and very finely sliced

25g (1oz) butter, cut into pieces

salt

freshly ground black pepper

In a large saucepan, stir together the cream, milk, nutmeg, garlic and some salt and pepper, then taste and add more seasoning if needed, being fairly generous with the salt in particular as the potatoes will absorb a lot.

Bring the cream up to just below boiling, then add the sliced potatoes one slice at a time, so that each slice is coated in cream. Stir gently, then cook on the lowest possible heat for 4–5 minutes, so that the potato starch begins to meld with the cream (this helps prevent the cream splitting). Remove from the heat and leave to sit for 15 minutes.

Preheat the oven to 160°C (325°F), gas mark 3. Dot the bottom of a large gratin dish (ours is 30x22cm/12x8½ inches) with the butter, then use tongs to arrange the potatoes in the dish, laying the slices horizontally and tightly packing them into the dish. Press down firmly to remove any gaps between the layers. Pour over the hot cream mixture, but be careful not to overfill the dish. Bake the gratin for 1 hour.

After an hour, test for done-ness by inserting a sharp knife into the centre of the dish – you shouldn't feel much resistance. If it needs more time, return to the oven for up to 30 minutes, but check every 10 minutes. If the top is browning too fast, cover with a sheet of foil.

Leave to stand for 10 minutes before serving.

Creamy baked leeks

In this recipe, leeks are cooked slowly in cream and cheese until soft and golden. If your oven is running too hot, the cream may split – this doesn't matter at all in terms of how it tastes, it simply results in a slightly less pretty dish.

GET AHEAD Steam, cover and chill the leeks a day before you want to cook this.

Serves 6
Takes 1 hour 5 minutes

4 big leeks, roots and green parts trimmed away, tough outer leaves removed

200ml (7fl oz) double cream

2 tablespoons full-fat crème fraîche

a generous pinch of cayenne pepper

a pinch of salt

1 tablespoon Dijon mustard

a knob of butter

1 tablespoon plain flour

200ml (7fl oz) milk

flavourless oil, for greasing

100g (3½oz) Cheddar cheese, finely grated

freshly ground black pepper

Cut the leeks into roughly 5cm (2 inch) lengths, then halve lengthways down the middle. Wash well to remove any grit or soil, but try not to let the layers of leek come apart too much.

Set a steamer basket over a pan of simmering water. Add the leeks and steam them for 8 minutes. Meanwhile, whisk together the cream, crème fraîche, cayenne, salt, pepper and mustard, making sure the mustard is completely combined into the sauce.

Place a pan large enough to take the cream mixture over a medium heat. Add the butter and when melted add the flour. Cook for a minute, stirring to form a paste, then gradually add the milk, until you have a smooth sauce. Remove from the heat and whisk in the cream mixture, beating until absolutely smooth.

Preheat the oven to 170°C (335°F), gas mark 3–4, and grease a medium-sized ovenproof dish (ours is 24x18cm/9½x7 inches) with oil. Arrange the leeks in more or less a single layer in it, cut sides facing up. Sprinkle over one-third of the cheese. Pour the cream mixture evenly over the leeks, opening up the layers to ease the cream between them, then sprinkle over the rest of the cheese.

Place in the oven and bake for 40 minutes. If the leeks on top seem to be browning too fast, place a sheet of foil over the top of the dish, but don't cut the cooking time as the leeks need it to become tender.

Roast butternut and pomegranate salad

This is similar to one of our winter deli salads, a beautiful squash salad designed by Ginger Pig group head chef, Yvonne Hunter. It also works a vegetarian main course, or you could make it suitable for vegans by leaving out the feta. If you like, you can roast the peppers from scratch, over a gas ring or under the grill.

GET AHEAD Roast the butternut a day ahead, then chill; bring up to room temperature before adding to the salad.

Serves 4–6 with other dishes, or 2 as a main

Takes 35 minutes

1 butternut squash, about 650g (1lb 7oz), peeled, deseeded and diced into 2cm (¾ inch) chunks

2 tablespoons olive oil

leaves from 4 bushy sprigs of mint, finely sliced

leaves from ½ small bunch of parsley, chopped

a handful of rocket, watercress or any bitter salad leaves

2 roasted red peppers from a jar (in oil, not brine), drained and thinly sliced

3 spring onions, finely sliced

seeds from ½ pomegranate

juice of ½ lime

1 tablespoon extra virgin olive oil

50g (1¾oz) feta cheese, crumbled (optional)

salt

freshly ground black pepper

Preheat the oven to 200°C (400°F), gas mark 6. Line a roasting tin with baking paper. Add the butternut and then spoon over the olive oil and add some salt and pepper. Use your hands to toss and coat each piece in oil. Place in the oven and roast for 20 minutes, or until tender. Remove from the oven and set aside to cool.

In a large bowl, toss together the butternut with all the herbs, vegetables and the pomegranate seeds, then add the lime juice, extra virgin olive oil, a pinch of salt and some pepper. Toss gently to coat. Strew the salad over a large serving platter and then scatter over the feta, if using. Serve straight away.

Celeriac remoulade

Knobbly, muddy celeriac is no looker, but it's hiding some serious flavour – peppery and nutty, with a hint of its cousin celery, all of which come to the fore when you shred and tumble it with soured cream and mustard. In France, celeriac remoulade is commonly served as a starter (and also in one of Rebecca's favourite restaurants, Brasserie Zédel, in Piccadilly, where it is shaped into a neat mound on each small plate), but it makes an excellent side to a cold-cuts lunch.

Optional extras to serve over or alongside remoulade include chopped dill, chopped parsley, toasted walnuts, cured or cooked ham (see page 94), or hot- or cold-smoked fish.

Serves 8 as a starter or 6 as a salad or side
Takes 15 minutes

1 celeriac, about 800g (1lb 12oz), peeled

3 heaped tablespoons good-quality mayonnaise

2 tablespoons soured cream

2 teaspoons wholegrain mustard

2 heaped teaspoons smooth Dijon mustard

2 teaspoons lemon juice

1 teaspoon sherry vinegar or red wine vinegar

salt

Grate the celeriac using the coarse side of a box grater, or shred it using a mandolin or the grater attachment on a food processor. Place in a bowl and then add all the other ingredients. Stir well, then taste to check the seasoning and add a pinch of salt, as needed. Serve straight away, or store in the refrigerator for up to 3 days.

Ginger Pig sprout and fennel slaw

This is a great way to make use of any extra sprouts, while also having something crunchy and zingy to serve with cold cuts or cheese.

Serves 4–6
Takes 15 minutes

150g (5½oz) Brussels sprouts, trimmed and shredded

1 carrot, julienned or grated

¼ red cabbage, 100g (3½oz), cored and shredded

2 tablespoons finely chopped dill

2 tablespoons finely chopped mint

4 tablespoons roughly chopped parsley

¼ fennel bulb, finely julienned

½ red onion or 3 shallots, finely sliced

For the vinaigrette

1 tablespoon Dijon mustard

1 teaspoon cider vinegar

1 teaspoon honey

zest of ½ orange

juice of 1 orange

3 tablespoons extra virgin olive oil

salt and freshly ground black pepper

Whisk together the vinaigrette ingredients, then taste to check that it's a good balance of sweet, tart and slightly salty. Place all the slaw ingredients in a large bowl and add half the dressing. Toss. Add more dressing as needed – you want it to coat the vegetables, but not make the slaw wet. Serve straight away or refrigerate for 1–2 hours until needed. Bring up to room temperature before serving.

Ginger Pig red cabbage slaw

This is the Christmas slaw we serve in the Ginger Pig delis and it's a crunchy, fresh alternative to cooked red cabbage. It will keep in the refrigerator for several days and is excellent as part of a Boxing Day lunch. (If you're making the pulled meat buns on page 137, you could use some of this slaw mixed with some mayonnaise, as part of the filling.) Bring up to room temperature before serving, especially if other sides are warm.

Serves 8–10
Takes 15 minutes

½ red cabbage, 200–250g (7–9oz), cored and shredded

125g (4½oz) whole raw beetroot, peeled and coarsely grated

50g (1¾oz) dried cranberries

zest and juice of ½ orange

2 tablespoons sunflower oil (or a mild-tasting extra virgin olive oil)

2 teaspoons red wine vinegar, plus more to taste

salt

freshly ground black pepper

Place all the ingredients into a large bowl, and toss together. Taste and add more vinegar, salt or pepper, as needed.

Spiced braised red cabbage

This is a slow-cooked, buttery and gently spiced red cabbage.

 GET AHEAD Prep the vegetables a day in advance and store in the pan, in the refrigerator, with all the spices, until ready to cook.

Serves 6–8
Takes 1¼ hours

1 small red cabbage, about 400g (14oz), cored and shredded

2 small red onions, finely sliced

2 pears, peeled, cored and diced

150ml (¼ pint) sweet cider

a generous pinch of ground allspice

a generous pinch of ground cloves

a generous pinch of ground cinnamon

4 juniper berries, lightly crushed

zest of ¼ lemon

2 tablespoons brown sugar

2 tablespoons red wine vinegar

a generous knob of butter, plus more to serve

a very generous pinch of salt

freshly ground black pepper

Place everything in a large heavy-based pan with a lid. Bring up to a gentle boil, then cover and simmer for 1 hour, or until the cabbage is very tender. Taste – the cabbage should be rich and silky, so if there's a lot of liquid, remove the lid, increase the heat and let bubble away. Add another knob of butter just before serving and season generously.

Greens with lemon and black pepper

When Rebecca suggested making this with kale, Tim said that he prefers to feed his kale to the cows. It works with any greens, bringing fresh green flavours to the Christmas table – choose your favourite (but not kale, if you're cooking for Tim).

Serves 6
Takes 15 minutes

375g (13oz) cavolo nero, kale, baby kale, hispi or Tenderstem broccoli

a knob of butter or 1 tablespoon extra virgin olive oil

lemon juice, for squeezing

salt

freshly ground black pepper

If using kale or cabbage, remove any tough stems and finely slice the leaves, unless using baby kale. If using broccoli, trim the stems and halve any very thick ones.

You can either steam the greens over a pan of simmering water in a steamer basket, or you can cook them in a pan. Either way, they will need just a few minutes of cooking. If using a steamer, you can set it over a pan in which you are cooking something else, to save both time and space. If not, set up the steamer with some simmering water, add the vegetables and cook for 3–4 minutes, or until tender – don't let broccoli become soft. If using a pan, cook with just a splash of boiling water, covered, for 3–4 minutes.

Drain away the excess water, then add the butter or extra virgin olive oil, a small squeeze of lemon juice, a small pinch of salt and lots of black pepper. Taste and add more lemon, if liked. Keep warm until ready to serve.

Bread sauce

Tim loves bread sauce – he says you cannot add too much butter (he uses more than we do here). He remembers eating cold bread sauce, known as 'pobs', in sandwiches as a child growing up in Worksop. Pobs is a northern dish that goes back to medieval times – a comforting dish of bread soaked in milk.

GET AHEAD Bread sauce freezes well, or can be made a day ahead. Reheat with a little extra milk if too thick.

Serves 6
Takes 10 minutes, plus 15 minutes infusing

375ml (13fl oz) milk

½ onion

1 bay leaf

1 clove

a pinch of freshly grated nutmeg

a pinch of salt

a pinch of white pepper

50–60g (1¾–2¼oz) fresh white or panko breadcrumbs

a very generous knob of butter

Place everything except the breadcrumbs and butter in a pan and bring up to a gentle simmer, stirring often so the bottom doesn't catch. Remove from the heat, cover and leave to infuse for 15 minutes.

Fish out the onion, bay leaf and clove. Add 50g (1¾oz) of the breadcrumbs, return to the heat and stir gently to form a thick sauce, adding the rest of the breadcrumbs if you feel it is too loose. Add the butter and stir well. Taste and add more salt or pepper, if needed, remembering it's meant to be a gentle, mellow sauce. Serve warm.

Horseradish sauce

If you've chosen rib of beef for Christmas Day, nothing beats serving homemade horseradish sauce alongside it. Ideally, make this the day before and let the flavours come together overnight. To grate horseradish, use a microplane or the finest setting of your grater to ensure a smooth result. Find horseradish root in speciality grocers, online or in some larger supermarkets. In this quantity, it won't cause you any bother, unless you sniff it, but deli head chef Gemma Aston once forgot to put on the extractor while making horseradish sauce by the kilo and nearly blew the heads off the whole team.

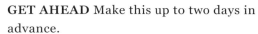

GET AHEAD Make this up to two days in advance.

Serves 8
Takes 5 minutes, plus 15 minutes infusing

30g (1oz) freshly grated horseradish root

1½ teaspoons white wine vinegar

1 teaspoon Dijon mustard, plus more to taste as needed

75ml (5 tablespoons) crème fraîche, plus more as needed

75ml (5 tablespoons) double cream, plus more as needed

salt and white pepper

Mix everything together with a pinch of salt and white pepper. Leave to infuse for 15 minutes, or overnight, then taste. If the horseradish flavour is too strong, add equal amounts of cream and crème fraîche until the pepperiness is to your taste. Alternatively, add more mustard, salt or white pepper to taste. Chill in the refrigerator until about 30 minutes before you are ready to serve.

Ginger Pig poultry gravy

In our shops, where we sell it freshly made, we call this turkey gravy, but you can make it for any bird. If you have leftover gravy, keep it in the refrigerator and use it in our shepherd's pie on page 138.

If you don't have the giblets from your bird, or if you want to make the stock for the gravy in advance, you could simmer chicken wings, or the bones from a roast chicken or goose, instead – we cook our goose legs separately, a day ahead, meaning there are bones to be roasted for stock (see page 78). Either freeze the bones until you want to make stock, or use a carcass to make 1.5 litres (2¾ pints) of stock a few weeks ahead, and then freeze that.

 GET AHEAD Make a day or two early, or several weeks early if using bones from a roast chicken, and store in the freezer.

Serves 6
Takes 2 hours

poultry giblets (the neck, heart and gizzard – not the liver)	5 peppercorns
1.5 litres (2¾ pints) water	150ml (¼ pint) white wine
1 carrot, chopped	1 heaped teaspoon cornflour (optional)
1 onion, chopped	Dijon mustard (optional)
a handful of flat leaf parsley	salt
1 bay leaf	freshly ground black pepper

While your bird is roasting, gently simmer the giblets in the water, with the carrot, onion, parsley, bay leaf and peppercorns for 1½ hours before straining out and discarding the solids. Next, bring up to the boil and reduce the liquid by half.

Once the bird is cooked and resting separately, spoon off the fat, then place the roasting tin in which it was cooked over a medium heat on the hob. Add the wine to the tin and use it to deglaze, scraping off any stuck-on bits as you go. Add the reduced stock and simmer for 5 minutes.

If you'd like a thicker gravy, combine the cornflour with just enough hot water to loosen it, pour into the simmering gravy and mix well until thickened. Cook for a couple of minutes, then taste to check that no chalkiness remains from the cornflour.

Season to taste and add a dollop of Dijon mustard, if you like. (We do!) Pour into a gravy jug, sieving out any solids that remain, if necessary.

Ginger Pig red wine gravy

This unctuous gravy is for red meats. It sounds more complex than it really is, and it is entirely worth the effort.

GET AHEAD Make this up to a month in advance, and freeze it.

Serves 6
Takes 2 hours, plus 20 minutes infusing

500g (1lb 2oz) raw beef bones, including some marrow and ribs, cut into 10cm (4 inch) pieces

150g (5½oz) raw chicken wings, including wing tips, or 1–2 raw chicken carcasses

300ml (½ pint) red wine

1.5 litres (2¾ pints) homemade or fresh beef stock (not from a cube)

1 tablespoon redcurrant jelly

3 flat leaf parsley stalks

2–3 teaspoons cornflour (optional)

salt

freshly ground black pepper

Preheat the oven to 200°C (400°F), gas mark 6. Place the beef bones and chicken wings or carcasses in a roasting tin and cook in the hot oven for 30 minutes, or until dark brown all over. Remove from the oven and place the bones in a large saucepan.

Set the roasting tin over a medium heat on the hob and pour in the wine. Deglaze the tin, scraping any stuck-on bits off the bottom, then pour this mixture into the saucepan.

Set the pan over a medium heat. Add the beef stock and redcurrant jelly, bring up to a rolling boil and then reduce for about 1 hour, or until the gravy has a thick, glazed appearance. Use a spoon to skim off any scum from the surface. Remove from the heat, add the parsley stalks and leave to infuse for 20 minutes.

Strain out the solids, then spoon any excess fat from the surface or pour the gravy into a fat-separating jug. Measure the gravy – if it has reduced to less than 400ml (14fl oz), top it up with a little hot water, unless you want less, but very concentrated, gravy.

Once the fat has been removed, you can thicken the gravy with a little cornflour, if you like: stir a couple of tablespoons of the gravy into the cornflour until smooth. Return the gravy to the pan and bring up to a simmer. Add the cornflour mixture and cook for 3–4 minutes, stirring, until thickened. Taste and adjust the seasoning – if you used shop-bought fresh stock, you may not need any salt. Serve the gravy warm.

Cranberry port sauce

Pair this not just with the usual turkey, but also with roast pork, either hot
or cold.

GET AHEAD You can make this months in advance. Keep in jars, in a cool,
dark place.

Makes 2 x 400g (14oz) jars
Takes 45 minutes

200g (7oz) soft dark brown sugar	zest and juice of 1 orange
50ml (2fl oz) water	1 cinnamon stick
50ml (2fl oz) port	
500g (1lb 2oz) fresh or defrosted frozen cranberries	

If making to store or give away as gifts, sterilize the jars following the instructions on
pages 42–3.

Place a deep pan over a low-medium heat and add the sugar, water and port, stirring to
dissolve the sugar. Add the rest of the ingredients and simmer gently for 20 minutes,
breaking the cranberries down with a potato masher. Cook gently until thickened and
saucy, about 15 minutes.

Remove from the heat and discard the cinnamon stick. If storing in jars, carefully pour
the hot sauce into the prepared jars, cover each snugly with a
lid, and store in a cool, dark place until ready to use. If
using in the next few days, pour into a bowl or tub,
cover and store in the refrigerator.

Redcurrant jelly

You will need to prepare 2–3 jars for this jelly. (It's hard to say exactly how many as it depends on how much juice you get from the fruit.)

 GET AHEAD Make this months ahead of Christmas and store in a cool, dark place.

Makes 2–3 x 400g (14 oz) jars
Takes 50 minutes, plus overnight straining

1kg (2lb 4oz) fresh or defrosted frozen redcurrants

300ml (½ pint) water

caster or granulated sugar

Place the redcurrants in a saucepan, first removing any damaged fruits or bits of twig, if fresh. Run a fork's tines down the stems to detach the fruit, if still attached.

Add the water to the pan, then bring up to the boil and simmer until the redcurrants are soft. Gently mash with a potato masher, then simmer for a further 20 minutes.

Strain the mixture overnight through a jelly cloth set over a large bowl. Next day, squeeze the remaining juice from the bag, but don't press too hard, as it may make the jelly cloudy.

If making to store or give away as gifts, sterilize the jars following the instructions on pages 42–3.

Weigh the liquid, then weigh out the same amount of sugar – that is, add 500g (1lb 2oz) of sugar to 500g (1lb 2oz) of liquid. Place both in a pan set over a medium heat. Stir until the sugar dissolves, then bring up to a rolling boil, skimming off any foam that gathers on the top of the jelly.

The jelly needs to reach a setting point of 105°C (221°F). If you have a jam thermometer, use it to judge when this is reached. If not, place a small plate into the freezer. When the jelly looks as though it is thickening and the boil isn't so vigorous, place a drop onto the chilled plate, leave for a moment, then tilt the plate. If the jelly runs down the plate, keep boiling and return the plate to the freezer for another test. If it sets onto the plate, then the setting point has been reached.

Strain the jelly through a fine sieve. If storing in jars, carefully pour the hot jelly into the prepared jars, cover snugly with a lid, and store in a cool, dark place until ready to use. If using in the next few days, pour into a bowl or tub, cover and store in the refrigerator.

Piccalilli

Piccalilli needs time to mature, so make this 4–6 weeks before Christmas if you want to eat it with your ham (see page 94). If you're making it as a Christmas gift, tell the lucky recipient to wait until February before diving in.

 GET AHEAD Make six months or even a year ahead.

Makes about 6 x 400g (14oz) jars
Takes 45 minutes, plus overnight salting

1 large courgette, about 400g (14oz)

1 small red pepper, deseeded

1 small yellow pepper, deseeded

125g (4½oz) fine green beans, trimmed

¼ small cauliflower, about 200g (7oz)

125g (4½oz) fresh or pickled silverskin or baby onions, peeled and halved

40g (1½oz) salt

400ml (14fl oz) cider vinegar

4 tablespoons cornflour

1 tablespoon ground turmeric

1 tablespoon English mustard powder

1 teaspoon cumin seeds

1½ teaspoons coriander seeds

1 tablespoon mustard seeds

125g (4½oz) granulated sugar

2 tablespoons honey

Cut all the vegetables, apart from the onions, into 1cm (½ inch) pieces. Place in a bowl (excluding the onions if they're pickled), sprinkle over the salt, toss well, cover and place in the refrigerator overnight.

The next day, rinse the vegetables really thoroughly, and leave to drain. If making to store or give away as gifts, sterilize the jars following the instructions on pages 42–3.

Make a paste with 75ml (2½fl oz) of the vinegar, the cornflour, turmeric, mustard powder, cumin seeds, coriander seeds and mustard seeds.

Place the rest of the vinegar in a large pan with 100ml (3½fl oz) water water, sugar and honey and bring up to the boil, stirring to completely dissolve the sugar. Spoon 3 tablespoons of the hot vinegar into the cornflour mixture and stir until smooth. Then pour the cornflour mixture into the pan, stirring as you do so. Bring back up to the boil and simmer for 6 minutes.

Stir the vegetables (including the onions) into the hot pickle mixture, then bring back to a simmer. Cook, stirring, for 3–4 minutes. Divide the hot piccalilli between the sterilized jars immediately, pressing the mixture down to make sure that no air bubbles remain (which can cause spoilage). Seal with the lids. Leave to mature somewhere dark and cool for 4–6 weeks. Once opened, store in the refrigerator and use within a couple of weeks.

Ginger Pig classic chutney

We make this chutney by hand in our Loughton kitchens. You'll find it very good with cold meats, cheeses and pies. Chutney needs time for the flavours to develop, so make this ahead of Christmas itself and store in sterilized jars.

GET AHEAD Make three months to a year in advance.

Makes about 7 x 400g (14oz) jars
Takes 2½ hours, plus overnight soaking

250g (9oz) dates, pitted and chopped

250g (9oz) raisins

500ml (18fl oz) malt vinegar

50ml (2fl oz) water

1 tablespoon sunflower oil

4 onions, diced

250g (9oz) soft brown sugar

3 large Bramley apples, about 750g (1lb 10oz), peeled and diced

100g (3½oz) tinned chopped tomatoes

1 tablespoon ground ginger

½ teaspoon ground cloves

Soak the dried fruit in the vinegar and water overnight.

If making to store or give away as gifts, sterilize the jars following the instructions on pages 42–3.

Place a large saucepan over a low-medium heat. Add the oil and when hot, add the onions and cook, stirring often, until soft – do not allow to brown.

Pour the fruit and vinegar mixture into the pan and add the sugar, apples, tomatoes, ginger and cloves. Stir well to help the sugar dissolve, then bring up to a simmer and cook, stirring often, for 2 hours, or until thickened and pulpy. Carefully pour the hot chutney into the prepared jars, cover snugly with a lid, and store in a cool, dark place for at least 4 weeks (but ideally 8–12 weeks) before serving. Once opened, store in the refrigerator and use within a couple of weeks.

IDEAS FOR LEFTOVERS

Freezing leftover meat means you can use it up over the next month or so. Strip the meat from the bones of your birds and tear or chop it into bite-sized pieces; slice up roast pork, discarding the stuffing and excess fat; even ham can be frozen, either as a piece or chopped into lardons to use in things like carbonara or to add to soups. Got leftover cooked veg? Freeze that too, for bubble and squeak, for soups, or for curries. All the suggestions on page 129 serve 4.

Ragù

Duck, goose, guinea fowl and pork all make a delicious ragù for pasta. Finely dice an onion and fry until soft and golden. Add a crushed clove of garlic and a pinch of fennel seeds and cook for a minute, then add two tablespoons of tomato purée, half a glass of red wine and 200ml (7fl oz) or so of passata. Let bubble for five minutes. Next, add three handfuls of shredded pork or duck, and cook the whole thing down for half an hour or so, stirring often and adding splashes of water if the sauce looks at all dry. You could also add some fresh or dried chillies, or a scoop of spicy 'nduja paste. The ragù is ready when thick and saucy. Taste and season with salt and pepper. Serve tossed into pasta or gnocchi.

Risotto

Cook a diced onion and a pinch of salt in a knob of butter until translucent. Add 300g (10½oz) of risotto rice and toss in the butter. Add 125ml (4fl oz) of white wine and allow to bubble away. Next, add 1 litre (1¾ pints) of hot chicken or vegetable stock, a ladleful at a time, stirring and allowing each spoonful to be absorbed before adding another. The risotto is done when the rice is tender (but not mushy) and the risotto is creamy. Season with a knob of cold butter and some more salt and black pepper. Add leftover cooked poultry and heat it through thoroughly, along with your choice of: sautéed wild or chestnut mushrooms, with or without sautéed bacon; a handful of frozen peas or shelled broad beans (bacon is also welcome here); roasted squash with crispy sage leaves (see page 32); a handful of finely chopped fresh green herbs, like basil, tarragon and parsley; or sautéed courgette and lemon zest. Whatever you do, finish each plateful with lots of freshly grated Parmesan.

Pie

You could hand-make the puff pastry on page 34 (use half, freeze half, if so) or buy some good-quality all-butter puff, ready rolled. Make a béchamel by melting 50g (1¾oz) of butter with 75g (2¾oz) of plain flour, then slowly adding up to 500ml (18fl oz) of warm chicken or vegetable stock, until you have a smooth, fairly loose sauce. (Add your leftover poultry gravy too, if you have any.) Mix in a few handfuls of cooked shredded poultry meat, plus optional broccoli, peas, cooked spinach, tarragon, parsley, thyme or diced ham. A splash of cream is very good, too. Season, then pour the mixture into a greased pie dish and cover with a pastry lid. Brush with beaten egg, slice a vent hole in the centre of the pastry and bake for about 30 minutes at 180°C (350°F), gas mark 4, or until the pastry is puffed up and golden brown.

Puffs

If you've ever had one of our pork puffs from the deli counter, you'll already know why we love this recipe. Shred leftover roast pork until the texture of pulled pork, then add chilli jam, a pinch of ground star anise, hoisin sauce and finely chopped spring onions, until everything is combined into a thick saucy mixture. Enclose in rectangles of puff pastry, brush with egg yolk or beaten egg and bake at 180°C (350°F), gas mark 4, for 30 minutes, or until golden brown and puffed up. The principle is the same for all sorts of leftovers: roasted vegetables and blue cheese; diced ham with ricotta, lemon zest and chopped sage; or chicken or turkey with Taleggio and wilted spinach.

Boxing Day bubble and squeak

Sometimes, bubble and squeak is made with added mashed potato to help bind it, which we aren't adding here because on Boxing Day the whole point is using up leftovers, rather than cooking anything more from scratch. That makes this bubble a bit more like a hash, but that's fine by us.

Hollandaise makes this an extremely luxurious bubble and squeak. Our recipe on page 22 is so quick and easy to make and...well, it is Christmas.

Serves 2–3
Takes 25 minutes

75g (2¾oz) diced pancetta, bacon or ham (optional)	4–6 eggs
butter or flavourless oil, for frying	freshly made Hollandaise Sauce (see page 22)
2 spring onions, white parts diced, green parts sliced, separated	finely chopped chives and/or flat leaf parsley, to sprinkle
about 400g (14oz) leftover roast potatoes and roast vegetables	salt
about 125g (4½oz) leftover greens or cabbage, shredded	freshly ground black pepper

Set the oven to a low heat, and gently warm 2 or 3 plates in it. Place a large frying pan over a medium heat. If using, add the pancetta, bacon or ham and sauté briskly, until crisp. For the last couple of minutes of cooking, add the diced white parts of the spring onions and cook until slightly softened. (If you're not using meat, just sauté the spring onion in butter or flavourless cooking oil.) Remove from the heat and lift out the meat and onion, leaving the fat behind. Place in a large bowl with the green parts of the spring onions, the leftover potatoes and vegetables, the greens and some salt and pepper. Mix, then use a potato masher to roughly crush the potatoes and vegetables.

Place the frying pan back over the heat. When hot, add the vegetables to the pan and spread out, pressing the mixture down to form a fairly even layer. Cook without stirring until the vegetables begin to brown and caramelize on the bottom. Gently flip the mixture over – it won't hold together, don't worry – so that the top is on the bottom.

Meanwhile, poach a couple of eggs per person following the instructions on page 21.

When the bottom of the bubble and squeak is golden brown, remove from the heat and arrange a couple of spoonfuls of it on each warmed plate. Top with the poached eggs, a spoonful of hollandaise and a sprinkling of the chopped fresh herbs. Season with a little salt and some black pepper just before serving.

Chipotle chilli-cheese turkey quesadillas

Tex-Mex-style quesadillas are a fantastic vehicle for leftovers. We aren't giving you quantities here, because the whole point of leftovers is making use of what you have. Feel free to mix and match. Allow two or three 25cm (10 inch) flatbreads per person.

Takes 30 minutes

grated Cheddar cheese

leftover cooked turkey or chicken, finely shredded

finely chopped spring onions

soured cream, crème fraîche or thick double cream

finely chopped red chilli, deseeded or not (optional)

a squeeze of lime juice

chipotle paste

wheat tortillas or flatbread wraps

hot sauce, to serve

Optional extras in the tortilla

roughly chopped coriander leaves

sweetcorn, canned or frozen

cooked and drained black beans

leftover roast potatoes or roast vegetables, diced and warmed through

crumbled feta cheese

Optional extras on the side

salsa made from finely chopped tomatoes and shallot, lime juice, salt and finely diced red chilli

guacamole

lime wedges

slaw or green salad

You need a generous handful of filling for each tortilla. Grate at least an equal amount of Cheddar to the amount of leftover meat you're using and place both in a bowl with 1–2 finely chopped spring onions and just enough soured cream, crème fraîche or double cream to bind the mixture. Add the chilli, if using, a squeeze of lime juice and a little chipotle paste and mix well to combine. (Add any optional extras to the filling now, too.)

Place a wide frying pan over a medium-high heat. When hot, lay a tortilla in the pan, then place a generous handful of the filling mixture onto the tortilla and spread it out over one half of the flatbread. Fold the other half over to cover the filling. Repeat with another tortilla. Cook until the bottoms are golden, then gently flip over to cook the other sides. They are done when the filling is piping hot, the cheese is melting and the outsides are golden brown. Scoop out of the pan and cut into wedges. Repeat with more tortillas until all the filling is used up. Serve hot with hot sauce on the side for drizzling or dipping.

Turkey miso noodles

This is the kind of dish you can do with the last of the turkey leftovers, after all the guests have left, in that lovely liminal period between Christmas and New Year. You can use frozen cooked meat in this broth; just be sure it's piping hot before serving. If you don't have broccoli, use a handful of finely sliced spring greens or sweetheart cabbage, finely sliced raw Brussels sprouts, or a head of pak choi, leaves and stems separated, roughly chopped.

Serves 2
Takes 30 minutes

600ml (1 pint) water or 400ml (14fl oz) water and 200ml (7fl oz) homemade chicken or turkey stock

2 heaped teaspoons miso paste, plus more as needed

a small thumb of fresh root ginger, peeled and finely sliced

75g (2¾oz) dried noodles, ideally udon, but egg noodles or rice noodles work well

4–5 stems of purple sprouting or Tenderstem broccoli, sliced

150g (5½oz) leftover cooked turkey, duck or goose, roughly shredded

For the eggs

2 eggs

3 tablespoons soy sauce

3 tablespoons water

2 tablespoons mirin or 2 teaspoons sugar

To serve

finely chopped spring onion

pinch of toasted sesame seeds

hot sauce, ideally Sriracha

sesame oil

soy sauce

For the eggs, bring a pan of water up to a simmering boil. Lower in the eggs and cook for 7½ minutes, then remove and plunge into cold water. When cool enough to peel, remove the shells. Stir together the soy sauce, water and mirin or sugar in a small bowl, then place the eggs in this marinade. Set aside, turning them often so they turn an even brown colour as they marinate.

Bring the water or water and stock up to a simmer, then add the miso and ginger, whisking the miso in so that it dissolves into the broth. Taste and add more miso if needed. Add the noodles and cook for 4 minutes less than the packet instructions. Add the broccoli and meat and cook for a further 2 minutes. Remove from the heat and divide between 2 bowls.

Halve each egg and nestle it in the broth. Sprinkle over a little finely chopped spring onion and a pinch of sesame seeds. Then drizzle over a dash of hot sauce and sesame oil, and serve with soy sauce on the side.

VARIATION Pork and gochujang noodles

Rebecca ended up with lots of rather wonderful leftover roast pork while she was working on the porchetta recipes in this book, so she invented this dish as a way to use it up. Rather than using poultry as opposite, slice up about 200g (7oz) of leftover slow-cooked pork (discard the stuffing). Place a small frying pan over a low heat and cover the base with water. Add a splash of soy sauce and a pinch of Chinese five spice (this is a blend of ground star anise, fennel, cloves, cinnamon and either black or Szechuan pepper). Add the pork to this mixture and cover. Allow to simmer for about 5 minutes, letting the flavours infuse into the meat. Make the noodle broth exactly as opposite, but add a spoonful of spicy Korean gochujang paste, swirling it in to dissolve. (If you don't have gochujang, just use miso and maybe add a pinch of chilli flakes.) When ready to serve, place the hot spiced pork slices on top of the broth, just before eating.

Pulled turkey brioche buns

We say turkey, but you could do this with slow-cooked pork or shredded chicken. A squirt of hot sauce wouldn't be a bad idea on these. Actually, neither would a side of fries...

If you have any slaw leftover – like the Ginger Pig Sprout and Fennel Slaw (see page 119) or Red Cabbage Slaw (see page 118) – you could use it in place of or along with the slaw below, but do add a little mayo for creamy richness.

Serves 4
Takes 30 minutes

400g (14oz) leftover cooked turkey, chicken or slow-cooked pork, finely shredded using 2 forks

150ml (¼ pint) good-quality barbecue sauce

100ml (3½fl oz) water or homemade chicken or turkey stock

4 brioche burger buns

good-quality mayonnaise, for spreading

burger pickles (sweet pickled cucumbers), sliced

pickled jalapeños, sliced (optional)

For the slaw

100g (3½oz) finely shredded sweetheart, red or white cabbage, or even raw Brussels sprouts (very well shredded)

1 small carrot, peeled and very finely shredded

1 shallot or spring onion, very finely sliced

2 teaspoons cider vinegar, or more to taste

¼ teaspoon fine salt, or more to taste

¼ teaspoon sugar, or more to taste

1 tablespoon mayonnaise

freshly ground black pepper

Place the shredded meat, barbecue sauce and water or stock in a saucepan and set over a medium heat. Cook, stirring, until hot through. Keep warm.

Make the slaw by stirring all the ingredients together. Taste and add more vinegar, salt or sugar, if needed – it should be tangy, creamy and crisp.

Split the buns and lightly toast the cut sides. Smear each side lightly with mayonnaise. Place a portion of slaw onto a bun half, then top with hot pulled meat. Add a few slices of the pickles and jalapeños, if using, and then park the bun lid on top. Serve straight away.

Shepherd's pie

This, of course, is not a real shepherd's pie, which should be made with lamb rather than poultry. Semantics aside, we think it's rather good. And when you cook a turkey, goose or chicken, it's important to eat every last bit.

Serves 4–6
Takes 1 hour 10 minutes

flavourless oil, for frying and greasing

1 small onion, finely diced

1 small carrot, finely diced

50g (1¾oz) streaky bacon, finely chopped

300ml (½ pint) leftover gravy or gravy topped up with chicken stock

200ml (7fl oz) homemade or fresh chicken stock (not from a cube)

1 teaspoon wholegrain mustard

1 teaspoon Dijon mustard

50–75g (1¾–2¾oz) leftover cooked sausagemeat stuffing, crumbled into chunks

650g (1lb 7oz) leftover goose, duck, turkey or chicken, a mixture of dark and light meat, roughly diced (or you can use lamb)

1 tablespoon finely chopped flat leaf parsley

salt

freshly ground black pepper

For the topping

700g (1lb 9oz) floury potatoes (Maris Piper are good), peeled and cut into chunks

4 tablespoons cream (double, single or whipping)

For the topping, place a large pan of salted boiling water over a medium heat. Add the potatoes, bring back to a simmer and cook until tender, 12–13 minutes. Drain and leave to steam for just a couple of minutes. Return to the pan and mash thoroughly (don't allow to cool before mashing or the mash will be gluey). Stir through the cream, taste and season with a little salt, and set aside.

Preheat the oven to 200°C (400°F), gas mark 6.

Pour a splash of oil into a large heavy-based saucepan set over a medium heat. Add the onion, carrot and bacon and sauté, stirring often, until the onion is translucent. Stir together the gravy, stock and mustards, whisking to ensure they're well combined. Pour the mixture into the vegetable and bacon pan, then add the sausagemeat stuffing and leftover meat. Stir through the parsley. Bring up to a simmer. Taste. It probably won't need salt, but add a little along with some black pepper, if needed.

Grease a ceramic baking dish measuring roughly 24x18cm (9½x7 inches). Pour the meat mixture into the dish. Spoon the mashed potato over the top, then spread it out gently with the back of a spoon or a spatula. Rake a fork back and forth over the top of the mash to rough it up. Bake the pie for 30 minutes, or until bubbling hot and browned on top.

Turkey, chickpea and kale curry with pomegranate raita

Turkey curry may make you think of Bridget Jones's mother's post-Christmas buffet...but we promise, this isn't that. In the week between Christmas and New Year, we find ourselves craving spice, heat, green vegetables, and we don't particularly want to go food shopping either. With any luck, you'll have most of the ingredients for this in the cupboard, refrigerator or freezer already. (You can keep root ginger very happily in the freezer.) This recipe is pretty robust and very flexible, so if you don't have one or two of the spices, don't worry.

Pomegranate raita is a great way to use up any pomegranate lurking in the refrigerator after making Fig and Pomegranate Pavlova (see page 154) or Roast Butternut and Pomegranate Salad (see page 116), with its little bursts of fresh, tart sweetness, but you can skip it if you don't have any, and use diced cucumber instead. If you don't have cavolo nero, you could use a handful of kale or fresh or frozen whole leaf spinach, roughly chopped.

Takes 50 minutes
Serves 4

flavourless oil, for frying

½ teaspoon black mustard seeds

½ teaspoon cumin seeds

1 large onion, finely diced

a generous pinch of salt, plus more as needed

3 cloves of garlic, crushed

3cm (1¼ inches) of fresh root ginger, finely grated

1 tablespoon finely chopped red chilli

1 tablespoon tomato purée

½ teaspoon ground turmeric

1 teaspoon ground cumin

1 teaspoon ground coriander

¼–½ teaspoon hot chilli powder

300ml (½ pint) water

3cm (1¼ inch) piece of cinnamon stick

4 green cardamom pods

4 cloves

a generous knob of butter

400g (14oz) can chickpeas in water, drained but not rinsed

300g (10½oz) leftover cooked turkey, goose, chicken or duck meat, frozen or fresh, roughly shredded

4 leaves of cavolo nero, tough stems removed, finely sliced

freshly ground black pepper

For the pomegranate raita

5 heaped tablespoons plain or Greek-style yogurt

a pinch of ground cumin

1 tablespoon very finely chopped shallot or red onion

2 tablespoons pomegranate seeds, plus a few more to garnish

a generous pinch of salt

Place a large heavy-based pan over a medium heat. Add a splash of oil and then the mustard seeds. Let them cook in the hot fat until they start to crackle and pop, then add the cumin seeds and cook for 1 minute. Next, add the onion and cook until translucent and beginning to brown. Add the salt, garlic, ginger, fresh chilli and tomato purée. Cook for another minute, stirring. Working quickly, add all the dried spices and a good dose of black pepper and cook, stirring, just long enough to briefly toast the spices. Add the water, cinnamon stick, cardamom, cloves and the butter. Bring up to a simmer and then add the chickpeas and cooked meat.

Cover with a lid and leave to bubble gently for 20 minutes. Add the shredded cavolo nero, stir and cover again. Cook for a further 5 minutes, or until the cabbage is tender. Taste and add more salt or chilli powder, as needed. If the curry seems wet, remove the lid and allow to reduce for a few minutes. Remove the cinnamon stick, and any of the other whole spices, if you can find them.

Stir together the raita ingredients. Serve the curry with steamed rice and the pomegranate raita on the side, topped with a few more of the jewel-like seeds as a garnish.

Duck and orange salad

Because duck is a rich and fatty meat, we prefer eating it hot, rather than cold, which means thoroughly reheating it and crisping up the skin before making this winter salad. This also works nicely with goose, or shredded glazed ham (see page 94).

Serves 2
Takes 30 minutes

300g (10½oz) waxy potatoes, halved if large

250g (9oz) leftover roast duck, or as much as you have, including any skin

2 big handfuls of watercress

½ small fennel bulb, trimmed and finely sliced

leaves from ¼ small bunch of parsley

1 tablespoon finely chopped dill

½ orange, peeled and sliced into small pieces

For the dressing

juice and zest of ½ orange

2 tablespoons extra virgin olive oil

1 teaspoon cider vinegar

2 teaspoons wholegrain mustard

a pinch of salt

freshly ground black pepper

Preheat the oven to 200°C (400°F), gas mark 6, to be sure it's hot before the meat goes in.

Place the potatoes in a pan of salted boiling water. Bring back to the boil and simmer until tender, about 12 minutes.

Arrange the duck in a single layer in a roasting tin. Make sure any skin is on top of the meat, and facing upwards. Cover the dish tightly with foil. Place in the oven for 10 minutes, then remove the foil and return to the oven for 5 minutes, to start crisping the skin (the skin should protect the meat and prevent it drying out).

After 5 minutes, remove the tin from the oven and separate the skin and the meat. Pop the meat in a small bowl and add 2 tablespoons of the boiling water from the potatoes. Cover the bowl and set aside. Return the skin to the oven for a further 5 minutes.

Whisk together the dressing ingredients. Place the potatoes, watercress, fennel, parsley and dill in a large bowl. Pour over half the dressing and toss.

Remove the skin from the oven, place on a board and roughly chop, then toss it with a pinch of salt. Divide the salad between 2 shallow bowls, or arrange on a platter. Drain and add the duck meat, orange pieces and crispy skin. Drizzle over the remaining dressing and serve immediately.

Ginger Pig | Sides, Sauces and Leftovers   143

SANDWICHES

Again, we won't give you quantities here, as the whole point is to use up what you have, with what's already in the refrigerator. One top tip (as told to us by Max Halley, author of *Max's Sandwich Book: The Ultimate Guide to Creating Perfection Between Two Slices of Bread*, and almost certainly the world's leading sandwich expert) is, that in any sandwich you should use more mayonnaise than you think is socially acceptable. He also advocates adding crisps – for texture – wherever possible, and if not crisps, crispy fried onions from a packet. We've checked, and he's right, on both counts. Something we haven't all experimented with is cold bread sauce, which Tim refers to as 'pobs' and tells us is wonderful in a sandwich.

Experiment with the bread – sometimes sourdough is good, but sometimes it's too sturdy, or is full of holes, or it has too much flavour for the filling. Sometimes a sandwich calls out for soft white sliced, sometimes you'll want a bun, or a bagel...or even a slice of rye bread so you can use up that bit of leftover smoked salmon with a little soured cream, mayo or horseradish crème fraîche...

Here are a few of our favourites (we talked, very happily, about sandwiches for *quite* a long time while making this list).

- Tim's ultimate ham sandwich – white bloomer bread, thickly cut hand-sliced ham (very good quality), English mustard (freshly made from powder) or piccalilli (see page 126).

- Gemma's porchetta sandwich – sliced leftover porchetta (discard any stuffing), mayonnaise mixed with good-quality pesto, rocket and perhaps some celeriac remoulade (see page 118).

- Tim's prawn sandwich – small sustainable cooked prawns (peeled), 3 tablespoons of Hellmann's mayonnaise, 2 tablespoons of soured cream, a squeeze of lemon juice, the grated rind of the lemon and lots and lots of very finely chopped dill, all served on sourdough as an open sandwich (this is also nice dotted with fish roe, or with a layer of gravlax at the bottom).

- Sliced leftover pigs in blankets, sliced red onion and chutney.

- Chicken liver pâté with finely sliced sweet pickled onions.

- Turkey (or any poultry), mayo, redcurrant jelly, crispy onions or a layer of crisps, crumbled stuffing and then a layer of Gruyère, left open and melted under the grill.

- Crispy bacon, chilli jam, Ogleshield cheese (a melting cheese, similar to raclette) and rocket; then toast the sandwich (we also make this with slices of haggis, cooked until crisp in the bacon fat).

- Flatbreads with leftover lamb, turkey, goose or chicken warmed in a little gravy or stock, crispy fried garlic, pomegranate seeds, yogurt, zhoug or harissa, pickled vegetables, pickled chillies or pickled onions, and crumbled feta.

- Roast beef with Dijon mustard.

- Roast beef, crisp lettuce and celeriac remoulade (see page 118).

- Roast beef, sauerkraut, French's American mustard, sliced dill pickles and Swiss cheese or Gruyère (Cheddar also works).

- Roast beef with horseradish crème fraîche (see page 121), with or without added Cheddar cheese, and Sprout and Fennel Slaw (see page 118).

- Roast beef, pink pickled onions (from a jar), Cheddar cheese and lettuce.

SWEET THINGS AND PUDDINGS

Christmas pudding

A proper Christmas pud, designed to be made well in advance, wrapped and matured for several weeks. To make the puddings you will need two 600ml (1 pint) ceramic or glass pudding basins. You could also make one large pudding in a 1.2 litre (2 pint) basin – the cooking times remain the same, although reheating might take slightly longer. Alternatively, you can use plastic pudding basins, with lids.

 GET AHEAD Traditionally, Christmas puddings are made on Stir-Up Sunday, the last Sunday before Advent begins.

Makes 2 medium-sized Christmas puddings
Takes overnight soaking; 8 hours on Day 1; several weeks maturing, plus 1 hour on Day 2

75g (2¾oz) sultanas

100g (3½oz) raisins

125g (4½oz) currants

6 tablespoons Pedro Ximénez sherry (or brandy)

100g (3½oz) beef suet

50g (1¾oz) chopped candied peel

200g (7oz) soft brown sugar

75g (2¾oz) plain flour

½ teaspoon baking powder

zest of 1 orange

zest of 1 unwaxed lemon

25g (1oz) blanched almonds, chopped

1 cooking apple, cored and grated

½ teaspoon ground cinnamon

¼ teaspoon freshly grated nutmeg

1 teaspoon ground allspice

125g (4½oz) fresh breadcrumbs

125ml (4fl oz) stout

2 eggs

butter, for greasing

8 tablespoons brandy, plus extra to flambé

a sprig of holly, to serve

Place the sultanas, raisins and currants in a bowl with the sherry or brandy and leave the dried fruit to plump up, ideally overnight.

On the day you want to give the puds their initial steam (they get 2, the last just before serving), use your largest mixing bowl and combine the suet, candied peel, brown sugar, flour, baking powder, orange and lemon zest, chopped almonds, grated apple, all the spices, the soaked fruit and the breadcrumbs.

In a separate bowl, whisk the stout and the eggs, then tip into the fruit mixture and stir well. (If you're doing this on Stir-Up Sunday, traditionally everyone in the household gets a turn to stir, and to make a wish.)

Grease 2 x 600ml (1 pint) pudding basins with butter, and place a disc of greased baking paper in the bottom of each. Divide the pudding mixture between the basins, pressing it down as you go, so that the mixture is densely packed with no air bubbles.

Cover the top of each basin with 2 layers of baking paper, cut to overhang by 5cm (2 inches), and tie them in place with string. Then cover each basin tightly with foil as well. (Alternatively, use plastic basins with lids, but double-wrap with foil just in case the lids come loose.)

If you have a big enough steamer, cook both puddings in that: set them in the steamer over a pan of simmering water. If you don't, you can use a saucepan with a lid for each pudding, but keep the basins away from the bottom of the pan with a ring made out of scrunched-up foil, to act as a trivet. Fill the pans with boiling water until it reaches halfway up the side of each pudding. Bring the water back to the boil, then turn the heat right down and cover the pans with well-fitting lids. The water needs to simmer for the next 7½ hours, so check every now and then and top up as necessary, with freshly boiled water from the kettle.

Once cooked, turn the heat off and leave the puddings until cool enough to lift out of the pans. Leave to cool completely, then remove the wrappers and pour 4 tablespoons of brandy over each one. Re-cover with fresh baking paper and tie with fresh string.

Place in a cool, dark place and leave until needed.

To serve on Christmas Day, you will either need to steam the puddings again for about an hour (using the method above) to reheat, or if you've used a plastic or microwave-safe pudding basin, you can do it in the microwave: remove the paper and any foil and cover with an upturned microwave-safe plate. Microwave on full power for 4 minutes, then stand for 5 minutes, before microwaving again for 4 minutes, this time on low. (Microwaves vary, so this is just a rough guide – do check the pudding is piping hot throughout before serving.) Turn out each pud onto a serving plate with a rim.

To flambé the puds in the traditional way, warm a little brandy in a small saucepan. Turn down the lights. Pour most of the brandy over the pudding, holding back a little in a metal dessertspoon. Hold the spoon over the pudding. Use a match or lighter to set fire to the brandy in the spoon, then carefully – and quickly – pour it over the pudding, and the rest of the brandy will catch alight.

Serve with brandy butter (see page 151), brandy cream, custard, cream, ice cream and/or a sprinkling of caster sugar.

Brandy butter

We like this with salted butter, but if you prefer, you can make it with unsalted and then add fine salt, to taste.

GET AHEAD Make two or three days ahead of when you need it. Store in the refrigerator.

Serves 4
Takes 10 minutes

100g (3½oz) salted butter, softened

50g (1¾oz) icing sugar, or more to taste

1 tablespoon brandy, or more to taste

Beat together the butter and sugar, then add the brandy and beat well again to incorporate it. Taste. If you want it to be sweeter, or boozier, add more sugar or brandy. Cover and store in the refrigerator until ready to serve.

Brandy cream

Serves 4
Takes 10 minutes

3 tablespoons icing sugar

125g (4½oz) extra thick double cream

75g (2¾oz) mascarpone

2–3 tablespoons brandy

Whisk together the sugar, double cream, mascarpone and 2 tablespoons of the brandy. If using an electric whisk, it will thicken up quite quickly, so be sure not to over-beat, or you'll get clumpy, buttery cream. Taste and add the last tablespoon of brandy, if you like. Store in the refrigerator until ready to serve.

Spiced clementine cake

This gently spiced cake is a great alternative to traditional Christmas cake – and it happens to be both gluten and dairy free, too. Because it is drizzled with fragrant clementine syrup, it keeps well. Try to find organic clementines, if you can.

 GET AHEAD Bake two or three days before it's needed, or bake and freeze.

Serves 8
Takes 1 hour 40 minutes, plus 2 hours soaking

4 unwaxed clementines, about 250g (9oz), scrubbed

5 eggs

4 tablespoons mild-tasting extra virgin olive oil, plus more to grease

225g (8oz) caster sugar

275g (9¾oz) ground almonds

2 teaspoons baking powder (gluten free, if necessary)

¼ teaspoon ground cardamom (or the seeds from 8 green cardamom pods, ground to a powder)

¼ teaspoon ground cinnamon

¼ teaspoon ground allspice

For the candied clementines and syrup

4 unwaxed clementines, scrubbed

125ml (4fl oz) boiling water

125g (4½oz) caster sugar

Place the 4 clementines for the cake into a pan of boiling water and bring up to a simmer. Cook for 30 minutes, or until the clementines feel tender.

Remove from the water, slice in half round the middle and remove any pips, then place the whole clementines (skin included) into a food processor or blender and whizz until smooth.

Preheat the oven to 180°C (350°F), gas mark 4. Grease a 20cm (8 inch) springform or loose-based cake tin and line the bottom with baking paper.

Add all the other cake ingredients to the food processor with the clementines and blitz to combine. Pour the batter into the prepared tin and bake for 50–55 minutes, rotating the tin after 35 minutes to ensure the top browns evenly. Check the cake is done by inserting a skewer into the centre – it should come out just about clean.

While the cake is cooking, make the candied clementines. Slice each clementine as thinly as possible, discarding the stem end and the bottom. Cut each slice in half. Place in a small saucepan and add the freshly boiled water and sugar. Bring up to the boil, turn

down the heat and simmer for 10 minutes. Remove from the heat, then lift out the slices gently, using tongs, and set aside. Keep the syrup.

Remove the cake from the oven and allow to cool in the tin for 10 minutes. Slide a palette knife or spatula around the tin to ensure it hasn't stuck anywhere, then release the sides and remove the cake from the tin. Cool the cake on a rack, then remove the paper from the base and place the cake on a serving plate. Prick the cake all over with a cocktail stick. Spoon 2 or 3 tablespoons of the orange syrup over the cake, then arrange the clementine slices on top. Leave for 1–2 hours, or overnight, for the syrup to soak in before serving.

Keep the remaining clementine syrup – it's delicious mixed with tonic, or added to a gin and tonic with a slice of fresh orange, or swirled into yogurt.

Fig and pomegranate pavlova

Rebecca's dad, Dave, is king of pavlovas, and is so famed for them that they are regularly requested by friends and family. He even made a stack of pavlovas for her wedding. If you don't like pistachios, lightly toasted flaked almonds are just as good here. You can also tweak the fruits to suit your tastes and the seasons – in summer, use strawberries, raspberries or roasted peaches. Blood oranges, passionfruit and mango are also great with clouds of sweet meringue, or try cooked fruits like poached cherries or frozen mixed berries simmered with a little sugar, to spoon over the pavlova when cool.

The leftover egg yolks can be used up in the hollandaise on page 22.

 GET AHEAD You can make the meringue base a day or two in advance, but store uncovered, or it will lose its crunch.

Serves 6–8
Takes 1½ hours, plus cooling

3 egg whites	**For the topping**
175g (6oz) caster sugar	300ml (½ pint) whipping cream
½ teaspoon vanilla extract	5 ripe figs, quartered
½ teaspoon white wine vinegar	3 tablespoons pomegranate seeds
1 teaspoon cornflour	1 tablespoon roughly chopped pistachios
	1 teaspoon pomegranate molasses

Beat the egg whites in the bowl of a stand mixer or with an electric whisk until very firm. Starting spoonful by spoonful, add the sugar, whisking continuously. Once the sugar is all whisked in, and the meringue looks thick, smooth and glossy, add the vanilla extract and vinegar and sprinkle over the cornflour. Scrape the bottom and sides of the bowl just in case any sugar has sunk. Whisk for 1 minute longer.

Preheat the oven to 160°C (325°F), gas mark 3. Draw a 20cm (8 inch) circle on a piece of baking paper. Pour the meringue onto the paper and smooth out to fill the circle. Place in the oven and cook for 1 hour. Remove from the oven and set aside to cool – it will deflate a bit, but don't worry.

When ready to serve, whip the cream (if you have a powerful stand mixer, be very careful not to overwhip it, or you'll end up with lumpy cream, or butter). Spoon it over the meringue, then arrange the figs on top. Scatter over the pomegranate seeds and pistachios, then drizzle over the pomegranate molasses, being careful not to get it on the meringue. Serve straight away.

Chocolate panettone bread and butter pudding

This is quite rich, so is fine on its own, but it is also quite fabulous with a scoop of good-quality vanilla ice cream, melting on top. Variations include cherries soaked in kirsch instead of raisins, milk or white chocolate instead of or as well as dark, and pecans or blanched and roughly chopped hazelnuts on top.

Serves 6–8
Takes 45 minutes, plus 1 hour soaking and 10 minutes standing

butter, for greasing

4 tablespoons raisins

4 tablespoons sweet pudding wine, rum, Marsala, sweet sherry, brandy or spiced liqueur

4 eggs

400ml (14fl oz) double cream

200ml (7fl oz) milk

zest of ¼ orange

100g (3½oz) caster sugar

½ teaspoon vanilla extract

a pinch of freshly grated nutmeg

650g (1lb 7oz) panettone, cut into slices, then triangles

50g (1¾oz) dark chocolate, 70–85% cocoa solids, broken into pieces

demerara sugar, for sprinkling

Grease a medium-sized ovenproof dish (ours is 24x18cm/9½x7 inches). Mix together the raisins and alcohol and then leave to soak – 10 minutes is fine, an hour is better.

Whisk together the eggs, cream, milk, orange zest, caster sugar, vanilla extract and nutmeg.

Arrange the triangles of panettone in the greased dish, stacking them next to each other, slightly at an angle, with the corners sticking up. Pour over the egg-cream mixture, ensuring all of each piece gets a coating, and moving the pieces gently to allow the mixture to flow in between them. If the orange zest has settled to the bottom, be sure to scrape out the bowl and pour it into the pudding. Set aside to soak for 30 minutes.

When ready to cook, preheat the oven to 180°C (350°F), gas mark 4. Remove the raisins from the alcohol and tuck them between the panettone slices, scattering some on top. Tuck the pieces of chocolate between the slices too. Sprinkle the whole dish with demerara sugar, for a crunchy top.

Place in the oven and cook for 25 minutes, or until the top is golden brown and the middle is piping hot, but still creamy and squidgy. (If you prefer your pudding to be a little more set, cook for 5–10 minutes longer, covering the top with foil if browning too much.) Leave to stand for 5–10 minutes before serving.

Granny Joy's chocolate mousse

This chocolate mousse recipe is special. Every Christmas, Rebecca's family-by-marriage, the Joyces, meet up on 27 December, travelling from all over the country to be together. The Joyce family is big, so the gathering often involves 30 or 40 people. Everyone brings a dish, and this is always on the dessert table.

Nowadays, it's made by Gill, Rebecca's husband's aunt – she and her children, Sarah-Jane and JJ, make double or triple quantities, and there is never any left over. But the original recipe belonged to Granny Joy, who was the much-loved matriarch of the family until her death in 2012, aged 93. Joy had five children, who all went on to have between three and five children themselves, children who are now grown up, and Joy now has nine great-grandchildren. Joy made this chocolate mousse for her children on their birthdays, meaning it has been part of the Joyce family for at least 60 years. The original recipe has been lost to time, but may have come from an old *Good Housekeeping* cookbook.

All the sugar in this recipe comes from the chocolate, so choose a sweet one rather than a very dark one with a high level of cocoa solids, or the mousse will be bitter.

Serves 8
Takes 25 minutes, plus overnight chilling

350g (12oz) good-quality sweet dark chocolate

juice of 2 oranges (about 6 tablespoons)

finely grated zest of 1 orange

6 large eggs, separated

2 tablespoons cold water

a pinch of salt

Set a heatproof bowl over a pan of barely simmering water. Break up the chocolate and place it in the bowl along with the orange juice and zest. Allow the chocolate to melt, stirring often to incorporate the juice, and being careful that the water underneath doesn't get too hot, because if the chocolate overheats it will become grainy and impossible to use.

Remove the bowl from the heat and set aside for a few minutes to cool slightly. Beat the egg yolks with the cold water, then beat them into the warm chocolate.

Place the egg whites in a clean bowl or into the bowl of a stand mixer. Add a pinch of salt and then beat until they form firm peaks. Fold the egg whites and chocolate together gently, mixing until completely combined.

Spoon into a large serving bowl or individual glasses or ramekins. Chill overnight in the refrigerator before serving.

Irish coffee

You can swap the whiskey for any number of spirits or liqueurs – amaretto, cream liqueur, chocolate liqueur or crème de cacao, hazelnut liqueur, dark fruit or berry liqueur, orange liqueur, brandy, dark rum, aged tequila…

Serves 2
Takes 15 minutes

5 tablespoons whipping cream

300ml (½ pint) freshly brewed strong black coffee (can be decaf)

4 teaspoons brown sugar, plus more to taste

75ml (2½fl oz) whiskey (ideally Irish, but others work just as well), plus more to taste

6 whole coffee beans or freshly grated nutmeg, to decorate (optional)

Pour the whipping cream into a small bowl. Using a hand whisk, beat until soft and mousse-y. (A softer whip makes for a nicer drinking experience, so don't beat as for a pudding.) Alternatively, if you have a milk frother, you can whip it in that, instead.

Warm 2 heatproof glasses or mugs. Divide the coffee between the glasses, then the sugar and whiskey. Mix well, then taste – it should be gently boozy and fairly sweet. Add more whiskey or sugar, as needed. Carefully spoon the soft whipped cream on top of the coffee, decorate if you like, and serve immediately. Drink the coffee through the cream.

Luxe spiced hot chocolate

This is incredibly rich and practically serves as a pudding, so really you only want a double-espresso-sized amount. Of course, you could top it with whipped cream, or marshmallows, but it really is a treat as it is. It's dangerously good cooled to room temperature and then spooned over ice cream. All the spices are optional.

Serves 2
Takes 10 minutes

125ml (4fl oz) whole milk

75ml (2½fl oz) single cream

1 teaspoon caster sugar, plus more to taste

75g (2¾oz) dark chocolate, at least 75% cocoa solids, broken or chopped into small pieces

¼ teaspoon vanilla extract or vanilla bean paste

a pinch of ground ginger

a pinch of ground cinnamon

a pinch of chilli powder

Warm 2 heatproof glasses or mugs. Place the milk, cream and sugar in a small pan set over a medium heat and bring up to just below boiling. Remove from the heat. Add the chocolate and whisk until completely melted. If it looks grainy, return to a low heat and warm gently, stirring constantly, until totally smooth. Sprinkle over the vanilla and spices, then whisk again and serve. Add more sugar if you prefer it sweeter.

Tim's orange and Madeira trifle

This recipe is a combination of two that came from Tim's mum, Patricia, who did not use jelly but did make a proper confectioner's custard, or crème pâtissière. When Tim was a little boy, she made trifles with slices of Madeira cake, liberally spread with apricot jam and then popped into the bottom of the trifle dish. She doused the Madeira cake with brandy, then dotted tinned apricots around and among the cake slices before topping them with custard and cream. The other trifle was made using McVitie's ginger cake, broken into chunks and put in the bottom of the dish. Rum was then cascaded over the cake, followed by tangerines, custard and cream.

Tim loves to garnish his trifle with miniature chocolate bars, which we've riffed on here by decorating the top of the trifle with smashed up dark chocolate honeycomb. (We like a brand called Mighty Fine.) Add this just before serving as it will melt slightly — deliciously — into the whipped cream.

If you don't want to add alcohol, use a little more of the juice the mandarin segments came in or some apple juice. If you really love jelly, add a layer of orange jelly on top of the sponge — we experimented with making fresh orange jelly, but found it tricky to get a reliably good set, so would recommend orange jelly from a packet, which has a suitably retro flavour. If you make your trifle with jelly, you will need to allow the custard to cool a little or the jelly will melt. The custard will set slightly as it cools, but don't worry, just spread it over and cover any wobbly bits with the cream.

Serves 6–8
Takes 45 minutes, plus setting

275g (9¾oz) ready-made Madeira cake	**For the crème pâtissière**
4 tablespoons Madeira (or sweet sherry or Pedro Ximénez sherry)	500ml (18fl oz) milk
	seeds scraped from inside 1 vanilla pod
2 x 390g (13½oz) pots or cans mandarin oranges in pear juice	6 egg yolks
350ml (12fl oz) whipping cream	100g (3½oz) sugar
75g (2¾oz) honeycomb dipped in dark chocolate	2 tablespoons cornflour
	2 tablespoons plain flour
	zest of ½ orange

Slice the cake into 2x8cm (¾x3¼ inch) fingers. Use them to line the bottom of a trifle bowl, then spoon over the Madeira or sherry, drizzling it over to soak into each slice.

Drain the orange segments, reserving the juice in a jug. Arrange the oranges on top of the sponge, then spoon over 6 tablespoons of the reserved pear juice.

Next, make the crème pâtissière: heat the milk and vanilla seeds in a saucepan until just boiling – don't let it burn onto the bottom of the pan. Remove from the heat. Meanwhile, beat together the egg yolks, sugar and both flours until pale, creamy and smooth.

Pour the hot milk into the egg yolk mixture slowly, whisking as you do so. When completely combined, pour the mixture back into the milk pan (check first that no milk is burned onto the base of the pan as it will come off in flakes and mix into the custard). Return to the heat and continue to whisk as you bring it back to the boil, being careful to get into the corners of the pan so nothing sticks (use a spatula to do this if necessary). It will suddenly thicken – continue to whisk once it does, and allow it to cook for 1 minute. Remove from the heat and whisk in the orange zest. This custard sets quickly, so pour it straight over the oranges in the trifle bowl, even though it's hot. Set aside to cool and refrigerate until you're ready to top with the cream.

Whisk the cream until it forms soft peaks, then spoon it over the custard. Keeping the honeycomb in its packet, or wrapped in a clean tea towel, whack it a few times with a rolling pin, just enough to break it up. Just before serving, scatter the chocolate honeycomb over the top.

Citrus salad with thyme syrup

If you don't want to make the earthy and fragrant thyme syrup, this is also lovely with the clementine syrup on page 152 (which you could make with the peel from the oranges, below, rather than sliced whole fruit), or you can leave the salad undressed if you'd prefer the enlivening tartness of naked fruit. If you don't want syrup, fresh mint or basil leaves, roughly torn, are a great addition.

GET AHEAD Make the syrup and prepare the fruit a couple of hours before serving, then assemble at the last minute.

Serves 6
Takes 15 minutes

4 oranges (avoid really huge ones)	**For the syrup**
3 blood oranges (or 3 more regular ones)	leaves from 3 sprigs of thyme
4 tablespoons pomegranate seeds	75ml (2½fl oz) boiling water
4–5 tablespoons ricotta	75g (2¾oz) caster sugar

First, make the syrup: place the thyme leaves in a small jug, then add the freshly boiled water. Leave to stand for 5 minutes. Strain into a small pan, discarding the leaves, and add the sugar. Warm gently, stirring to allow the sugar to dissolve and form a syrup. Remove from the heat.

Slice the skin and pith from the oranges, then slice the flesh thinly. Arrange on a serving platter. Scatter over the pomegranate seeds. Dot the fruit with dollops of ricotta. Spoon over some of the syrup, and serve immediately.

Mince pies with rum pastry

Tim once found one of his chefs, Paul Hughes, making dozens of different mince pies. Believing that meat pies were more important, Tim asked him to stop. Two weeks later, he found the same chef still obsessing over mince pies and told him to stop, again. Two weeks after that, a magazine declared the Ginger Pig mince pies the best mince pies in London. We've since sold tens of thousands of them. These are based on that very recipe.

 GET AHEAD Make the pastry and freeze the bases, uncooked, in the tart trays, ready to be filled and baked. Cut out and freeze the lids separately.

Makes 18
Takes 1 hour 10 minutes, plus 30 minutes resting

250g (9oz) plain flour	2 tablespoons rum
125g (4½oz) chilled butter, cut into cubes, plus more to grease	400g (14oz) mincemeat (see page 166 for homemade mincemeat)
75g (2¾oz) icing sugar, plus more to serve	1 egg, beaten
¼ teaspoon fine salt	a splash of milk
2 egg yolks	

Place the flour and the butter in a large bowl and use your fingertips to rub them together until the mixture looks like breadcrumbs, or blitz in a food processor. Stir in the icing sugar and salt. In a small bowl, beat together the egg yolks and rum. Make a well in the flour mixture and pour in the egg mixture. Use a wooden spoon to gradually work the egg into the pastry. If it seems a bit dry and crumbly, add 1–2 tablespoons of cold water. Form the dough into a ball, wrap in clingfilm or place on a plate and under a small bowl, and rest it in the refrigerator for 30 minutes.

Preheat the oven to 180°C (350°F), gas mark 4. Gently roll out the pastry on a floured work surface, trying to flatten it rather than stretch, as if it stretches it may shrink back when in the hot oven. When the pastry is 2–3mm (⅛ inch) thick, cut out 18 x 8cm (3¼ inch) discs for the bases, and 18 x 7cm (2¾ inch) discs for the tops. As long as you don't overwork the pastry, you can pat the scraps back into a ball and reroll it, to cut out more bases and tops.

Place the bases into a greased tart tray (or 2), then add a heaped teaspoonful of mincemeat to each pie, filling them to roughly level with the rim of the pastry. (Don't overfill, or they will burst.)

Mix the beaten egg and milk together, then gently brush the rims of the pastry. Set a lid on each tart, gently pressing the edges together to seal. Brush the tops with egg wash and use the tip of a sharp knife to cut a small vent into each one. (You could also decorate the pies with pastry scraps cut into stars or leaf shapes.)

Place in the oven for 25–30 minutes, or until the pastry is golden and crisp, turning the tray(s) round once halfway through to ensure even browning. Remove from the oven and allow to cool in the trays for 10 minutes or so, then turn out and cool on a rack. Dust with icing sugar before serving.

Ginger Pig Mincemeat

This recipe probably makes more than you'll need, but it will keep until next year, and makes a lovely gift. Make you sure you store it in spotlessly clean, sterilized jars (see pages 42–3). You can use this mincemeat straight away, but it benefits from a few days or even weeks of maturing, if possible.

GET AHEAD Make up to a year in advance.

Makes 6 x 400g (14oz) jars
Takes 30 minutes

200g (7oz) cooking apples, cored, peeled and finely diced

200g (7oz) beef suet

300g (10½oz) raisins

300g (10½oz) chopped candied peel

200g (7oz) currants

200g (7oz) sultanas

zest and juice of 2 lemons

zest and juice of 1 orange

3 tablespoons rum

4 tablespoons brandy

8 teaspoons mixed spice

6 teaspoons ground cinnamon

½ teaspoon freshly grated nutmeg

300g (10½oz) soft dark brown sugar

If making to store or give away as gifts, sterilize the jars following the instructions on pages 42–3. Place all the ingredients in your largest saucepan (or 2 smaller ones), set over a medium heat. Stir often, allowing the suet and sugar to melt together, then cook, still stirring frequently, for 10 minutes.

Spoon into the prepared jars while the mincemeat is still hot. Seal and leave to cool before storing somewhere dark, cool and dry.

Almond cookies

These almond cookies are incredibly easy to make, work beautifully with coffee or can be served with ice cream as an impressive but simple dessert. They keep well, can be frozen and are great to have on hand if you're likely to have lots of guests dropping in. They also make excellent gifts.

GET AHEAD Make a couple of days before you need them and store in a tin, or make further ahead and store in the freezer.

Makes 30
Takes 45 minutes

3 egg whites	1½ teaspoons vanilla extract
300g (10½oz) ground almonds	4 tablespoons flaked almonds
300g (10½oz) caster sugar	

Line 2 large baking sheets with baking paper. Preheat the oven to 175°C (345°F), gas mark 4.

Whisk the egg whites until fluffy, then mix them with the ground almonds, sugar and vanilla to form a slightly sticky dough. Break off walnut-sized pieces and roll into 30 balls. Place on the baking sheets and press down lightly to form thick round cookies, leaving space between them as they will spread out a little. Press a few flaked almond pieces into the top of each cookie.

Place the trays in the oven and bake for about 20 minutes, or until light gold, turning the tray around for the last 5 minutes, so that the cookies brown evenly.

Remove from the oven and allow to cool on the baking sheets.
Once completely cool, store in a lidded tub or jar.

Christmas cake

This recipe is based on Rebecca's mother's recipe, itself based on a recipe in an old *Good Housekeeping* cookbook. Rebecca's mum, Hilary, now makes this cake very successfully with gluten-free flour.

 GET AHEAD Make the fruit cake up to three months ahead of Christmas. 'Feeding' it every two weeks with brandy helps preserve and mature it.

Makes a 20cm (8 inch) cake
Takes 4¾ hours

200g (7oz) currants	½ teaspoon baking powder
200g (7oz) sultanas	⅛ teaspoon fine salt
200g (7oz) raisins	¼ teaspoon freshly grated nutmeg
100g (3½oz) dried cranberries	½ teaspoon ground cinnamon
100g (3½oz) chopped candied peel	½ teaspoon ground mace
50g (1¾oz) glacé cherries, roughly chopped	½ teaspoon mixed spice
50g (1¾oz) chopped almonds (omit to make this nut free)	225g (8oz) butter, at room temperature
2 tablespoons ground almonds (omit to make this nut free)	225g (8oz) soft brown sugar
	1 tablespoon black treacle
zest of 1 orange	1 teaspoon vanilla extract
zest of 1 lemon	4 eggs, beaten
225g (8oz) plain flour	8 tablespoons brandy, plus more to 'feed' the cake (omit to make this alcohol free)

Line the base and sides of a 20cm (8 inch) loose-based or springform cake tin with 2 layers of baking paper. Then tie 4 layers of newspaper around the outside of the tin, using string to keep it in place. Preheat the oven to 140°C (275°F), gas mark 1.

Mix the fruit, nuts and citrus zests together in a large bowl. Separately, sift together the flour, baking powder, salt and spices. In another large bowl, beat together the butter, sugar, black treacle and vanilla extract until fluffy, then gradually beat in the eggs and half the brandy. If the mixture seems to split, add a tablespoon or so of the flour to stabilize it. Fold the flour mixture into the egg-butter mixture, then fold in the fruit.

Pour the batter into the prepared tin and smooth over the top with a spatula. Place in the oven, sitting on 4 layers of newspaper, and cook for 1½ hours. At this point, cover the

top with a triple layer of baking paper. Cut a hole in the centre of each sheet, about the size of a coin, to allow steam to escape. If using a fan oven, weigh the paper down with a couple of metal skewers lying crossways over the tin, but not touching the cake. Cook for a further 2¼ hours, checking for done-ness 20 minutes before the full cooking time has elapsed by sliding a metal skewer into the centre of the cake. It should come out clean. If not, return to the oven for 10 minutes before checking again.

Cool the cooked cake in the tin. Release the tin and remove all the paper. Set the cake on a plate, prick all over the top with a skewer or cocktail stick and spoon over the remaining brandy, letting it soak into the cake.

Wrap it in a double layer of baking paper, held in place with string (or rubber bands), then store in an airtight tin. If you've made the cake in advance, feeding it with alcohol will help it to store well – spoon over a couple of spoonfuls of brandy every 2 weeks or so.

For the marzipan

Takes 40 minutes, plus at least 24 hours drying

150g (5½oz) icing sugar

150g (5½oz) caster sugar

325g (11½oz) ground almonds

2 eggs, beaten thoroughly

1 teaspoon vanilla extract

1 tablespoon lemon juice

apricot jam, for brushing,
any lumps of fruit removed

Sift the sugars into a large bowl. Add the almonds. Add half the beaten eggs, the vanilla extract and the lemon juice. Mix together to form a dough, adding more egg as needed – you probably won't need all of it. Pat and knead the dough lightly with your hands, pushing it together to form a neat ball, but don't overwork it once it has come together.

Create a reasonably flat surface for the marzipan by trimming the risen top off the cake. Brush the outside of the cake with apricot jam.

Divide the marzipan into 2 balls. Measure the circumference of the cake – it should be about 63cm (25 inches) – and the height, which should be roughly 7cm (2¾ inches). Dust a clean work surface with icing sugar. Form one of the marzipan balls into a long sausage and roll out to form a rectangle as long as the circumference and as wide as the height. If the marzipan sticks, slide a palette knife underneath it, then gently lift the marzipan up and wrap it around the outside of the cake. Don't worry if it looks quite messy at this point. Pat and press the marzipan onto the cake. If it cracks, just patch it up.

Roll the other ball out to form a disc roughly the size of the top of the cake, dusting the work surface with more icing sugar. Use the palette knife to loosen and then lift the marzipan onto the cake. Press the lid onto the side piece, completely encasing the cake

and making sure no gaps remain. Use the palette knife to press and smooth the marzipan around the cake until smooth, creating a neat right angle where the lid meets the sides.

Set aside to dry for at least 24 hours and up to 3 days (cover with a clean tea towel after 24 hours, if leaving for longer).

For the royal icing

Takes 45 minutes, plus at least 24 hours drying

750g (1lb 10oz) icing sugar	1 teaspoon lemon juice
3 egg whites	1 teaspoon glycerine

Once the marzipan is dry, sift the icing sugar into the bowl of a stand mixer, into a food processor or into a large bowl. With the beaters or a whisk running slowly, add the egg whites and slowly beat or whisk the sugar into the eggs. Once combined, add the lemon juice and the glycerine and continue to mix until smooth. When you lift the beaters, the icing should form firm glossy peaks. If the icing is runny, add a little more sifted icing sugar. If it's too thick to spread, gradually add a tablespoon of water, or more, as needed.

Place the cake on a presentation plate or board. Use a palette knife to spread the cake thickly with icing. Royal icing is best suited to a rough finish, but the icing should be evenly spread over the top and sides, otherwise the cake will look wonky. Use the palette knife to smooth the icing and check for any areas where the cake peeks through. Arrange any decorations that should stick in the icing on top now, but wait until the icing is dry to wrap ribbons around the outside. Set aside to dry for 24 hours or so before serving.

If you have any leftover icing, you can thin it with a little water, place it in a piping bag, and use it to decorate Christmas cookies or gingerbread. Store in a covered bowl in the refrigerator, with a piece of clingfilm pressed over the top to stop it drying out.

INDEX

Acknowledgements

Tim Wilson

I would very much like to thank Yvonne Hunter and Gemma Aston, doyennes of the Ginger Pig cookery team, for their time and help in compiling many of our in-house recipes. Also, thanks must go to the wonderful team who prepare these delicious dishes day to day – Vida and Audra in Moxon Street, and the butchers who prepare the meat for them.

Time was of the essence in producing the *Ginger Pig Christmas Cook Book*, so a big thank you to Rebecca, who not only cooked and tried each recipe, but also calculated the correct amounts and cooking times, and then wrote them all down. Behind the scenes, Lynsey Coughlan, my fellow director, co-ordinated deliveries of the raw products to Rebecca and then latterly to the photo studio, where another fabulous team produced the great photographs for the book – all cooked properly, taking no shortcuts – thank you to everyone.

Rebecca Seal

Thank you, Tim, for allowing me free reign on the Ginger Pig's archive of recipes and for trusting me with them, as well as letting me create some new dishes, too. (I'm still especially proud of that bread and butter pudding.) Thanks to Yvonne Hunter, Gemma Aston and Lynsey Coughlan at the Ginger Pig, who all found time for me, despite my asking about turkeys, pickles and porchettas during their busiest time of year. Working with you all has been a delight from start to finish.

Thank you to photographer Sam A Harris, who did a truly wonderful job capturing both Christmas (in February) and the Ginger Pig's aesthetic, alongside Annie Rigg, food stylist extraordinaire, and Tabitha Hawkins, who sourced and styled all the beautiful props and helped write the pages on table decor. Thanks also to Hattie Baker, who assisted Annie, and Sam's assistant Beca Jones.

Thanks to Emma Hunt, of wine shippers Thorman Hunt, both for her Christmas wine wisdom and for sending us wine to use in the photographs; and to Patricia Michelson at La Fromagerie for lending us her knowledge of cheeses.

This is my ninth book with Octopus and as ever, the publishing team made everything run like very enjoyable clock-work. Huge thanks to the book's art director Juliette Norsworthy, editor Alex Stetter and to publisher Alison Starling for bringing me on to this lovely project in the first place. Thanks to Tim's agent, Anna Power, and to my agent, Antony Topping, for navigating the business side of things so swiftly, too. Thank you to Jo Smith, for copy editing, and Jo Murray for proofreading – both absolutely vital but rather unsung roles.

Thanks to my family – especially my daughters, Isla and Coralie, for tolerating my busy-ness. (Although everyone in the house – and indeed many of my neighbours – did rather well in terms of delicious food.) My husband, Steve, took up an awful lot of slack while I disappeared into multiple deadlines over several months (Steve: I really couldn't do this crazy job without your support). Finally, thanks to my parents, Dave and Hilary, who gave me so many happy Christmases as a child, and who not only fielded my many questions about marzipan, icing and cooking times, but also let me use some of our family Christmas recipes in this book, too.

An Hachette UK Company
www.hachette.co.uk

First published in 2023 by Mitchell Beazley, an imprint of Octopus Publishing Group Ltd, Carmelite House, 50 Victoria Embankment, London, EC4Y 0DZ
www.octopusbooks.co.uk

Text copyright © Tim Wilson 2023
Photography copyright © Sam A Harris 2023
Design and layouts copyright ©
Octopus Publishing Group Ltd 2023

The authors have asserted their moral rights.

A CIP catalogue record for this book is available from the British Library.

ISBN: 978 1 78472 919 6

Printed and bound in China
10 9 8 7 6 5 4 3 2 1

Publisher | Alison Starling

Art Director | Juliette Norsworthy

Senior Editor | Alex Stetter

Photographer | Sam A Harris

Home Economist | Annie Rigg

Props Stylist | Tabitha Hawkins

Illustrations | Lindsay Lewis

Senior Production Manager | Katherine Hockley